2018-2019

Multi-student Catholic Homeschool Planner

Copyright © 2018
All rights reserved.
ISBN-13: 978-1723385209
ISBN-10: 1723385204
Scripture taken from the Catholic Edition of the
Revised Standard Version of the Bible,
copyright © 1965, 1966
National Council of the Churches
of Christ in the United States of America.
Used by permission.
All rights reserved worldwide.

2018-2019 Multi-student Catholic Homeschool Planner

By Jennifer Harbor Rainey

"The first end I propose in our daily work is to do the will of God; secondly, to do it in the manner He wills it; and thirdly to do it because it is His will."

St. Elizabeth Ann Seton

We have many special jobs as homeschooling Moms. We raise the kids, maintain the house, cook the meals, kiss the boo-boos, and also teach our little blessings. It can be overwhelming to say the least.

To make the days go as smoothly as possible, it is important to schedule our time. This planner should help you to do just that.

This planner has:

- ✓ **Daily/weekly planning pages** where you can list all of your kids' daily assignments. These pages offer spaces for you to list saints and Bible verses that you will explore that week.
- ✓ **Monthly planning pages** where you can make a general list of what you would like to teach that month. These pages also have a calendar and selected feast days.
- ✓ **Grade charts** where you can write down quarterly and yearly grades.
- ✓ **Several lists** to document your curriculum, field trips, reading lists, goals for next year, and more.
- ✓ **Information on the Most Holy Rosary and the Sacred Heart Devotion** to encourage you and your family.
- ✓ **A list of common Catholic prayers** that will serve as a helpful list when teaching your young kids to recite the Our Father, Hail Mary, and other prayers.

I pray that this planner will help us all through the school year. May God bless you and your families.

Jennifer Rainey

Weekly Planning Pages

Week 1

Memory Scripture Verse

_____

_____

_____

Saint of the Week

_____

Patron of…

_____

I am thankful for…

_____

_____

_____

Grocery List

_____
_____
_____
_____
_____
_____
_____
_____
_____
_____
_____
_____
_____

Meal Planning

Sunday:
_____

Monday:
_____

Tuesday:
_____

Wednesday:
_____

Thursday:
_____

Friday:
_____

Saturday:
_____

"Don't imagine that, if you had a great deal of time, you would spend more of it in prayer. Get rid of that idea; it is no hindrance to prayer to spend your time well."

St. Teresa of Avila

Week 1: Monday, _____
(Date)

Name ___	Name ___	Name ___	Name ___	Name ___	Name ___
Math	Math	Math	Math	Math	Math
English	English	English	English	English	English
Religion	Religion	Religion	Religion	Religion	Religion
History/Social Studies	History/Social Studies	History/Social Studies	History/Social Studies	History/Social Studies	History/Social Studies
Science	Science	Science	Science	Science	Science

Week 1: Tuesday, _____
(Date)

Name	Name	Name	Name	Name	Name
Math	Math	Math	Math	Math	Math
English	English	English	English	English	English
Religion	Religion	Religion	Religion	Religion	Religion
History/Social Studies	History/Social Studies	History/Social Studies	History/Social Studies	History/Social Studies	History/Social Studies
Science	Science	Science	Science	Science	Science

Week 1: Wednesday, _____

(Date)

Name	Name	Name	Name	Name	Name
Math	Math	Math	Math	Math	Math
English	English	English	English	English	English
Religion	Religion	Religion	Religion	Religion	Religion
History/Social Studies	History/Social Studies	History/Social Studies	History/Social Studies	History/Social Studies	History/Social Studies
Science	Science	Science	Science	Science	Science

Week 1: Thursday, _____
(Date)

Name	Name	Name	Name	Name	Name
Math	Math	Math	Math	Math	Math
English	English	English	English	English	English
Religion	Religion	Religion	Religion	Religion	Religion
History/Social Studies	History/Social Studies	History/Social Studies	History/Social Studies	History/Social Studies	History/Social Studies
Science	Science	Science	Science	Science	Science

Week 1: Friday, _____
(Date)

Name	Name	Name	Name	Name	Name
Math	Math	Math	Math	Math	Math
English	English	English	English	English	English
Religion	Religion	Religion	Religion	Religion	Religion
History/Social Studies	History/Social Studies	History/Social Studies	History/Social Studies	History/Social Studies	History/Social Studies
Science	Science	Science	Science	Science	Science

Week 2

Memory Scripture Verse

_____

_____

_____

Saint of the Week

_____

Patron of…

_____

I am thankful for…

_____

_____

Grocery List

_____
_____
_____
_____
_____
_____
_____
_____
_____
_____
_____
_____
_____

Meal Planning

Sunday:
_____

Monday:
_____

Tuesday:
_____

Wednesday:
_____

Thursday:
_____

Friday:
_____

Saturday:
_____

"For God so loved the world that he gave his only Son, that whoever believes in him should not perish but have eternal life."

John 3:16

Week 2: Monday, _____
(Date)

Name	Name	Name	Name	Name	Name
Math	Math	Math	Math	Math	Math
English	English	English	English	English	English
Religion	Religion	Religion	Religion	Religion	Religion
History/Social Studies	History/Social Studies	History/Social Studies	History/Social Studies	History/Social Studies	History/Social Studies
Science	Science	Science	Science	Science	Science

Week 2: Tuesday, _____
(Date)

Name ___	Name ___	Name ___	Name ___	Name ___	Name ___
Math	Math	Math	Math	Math	Math
English	English	English	English	English	English
Religion	Religion	Religion	Religion	Religion	Religion
History/Social Studies	History/Social Studies	History/Social Studies	History/Social Studies	History/Social Studies	History/Social Studies
Science	Science	Science	Science	Science	Science

Week 2: Wednesday, _____
(Date)

Name	Name	Name	Name	Name	Name
Math	Math	Math	Math	Math	Math
English	English	English	English	English	English
Religion	Religion	Religion	Religion	Religion	Religion
History/Social Studies	History/Social Studies	History/Social Studies	History/Social Studies	History/Social Studies	History/Social Studies
Science	Science	Science	Science	Science	Science

Week 2: Thursday, _____

(Date)

Name	Name	Name	Name	Name	Name
Math	Math	Math	Math	Math	Math
English	English	English	English	English	English
Religion	Religion	Religion	Religion	Religion	Religion
History/Social Studies	History/Social Studies	History/Social Studies	History/Social Studies	History/Social Studies	History/Social Studies
Science	Science	Science	Science	Science	Science

Week 2: Friday, _____
(Date)

Name ___	Name ___	Name ___	Name ___	Name ___	Name ___
Math	Math	Math	Math	Math	Math
English	English	English	English	English	English
Religion	Religion	Religion	Religion	Religion	Religion
History/Social Studies	History/Social Studies	History/Social Studies	History/Social Studies	History/Social Studies	History/Social Studies
Science	Science	Science	Science	Science	Science

Week 3

Memory Scripture Verse

Saint of the Week

I am thankful for…

Patron of…

Grocery List

Meal Planning

Sunday:

Monday:

Tuesday:

Wednesday:

Thursday:

Friday:

Saturday:

"Love is shown more in deeds than in words."

St. Ignatius of Loyola

Week 3: Monday, _____
(Date)

Name	Name	Name	Name	Name	Name
Math	Math	Math	Math	Math	Math
English	English	English	English	English	English
Religion	Religion	Religion	Religion	Religion	Religion
History/Social Studies	History/Social Studies	History/Social Studies	History/Social Studies	History/Social Studies	History/Social Studies
Science	Science	Science	Science	Science	Science

Week 3: Tuesday, _____
(Date)

Name	Name	Name	Name	Name	Name
Math	Math	Math	Math	Math	Math
English	English	English	English	English	English
Religion	Religion	Religion	Religion	Religion	Religion
History/Social Studies	History/Social Studies	History/Social Studies	History/Social Studies	History/Social Studies	History/Social Studies
Science	Science	Science	Science	Science	Science

Week 3: Wednesday, _____
(Date)

Name	Name	Name	Name	Name	Name
Math	Math	Math	Math	Math	Math
English	English	English	English	English	English
Religion	Religion	Religion	Religion	Religion	Religion
History/Social Studies	History/Social Studies	History/Social Studies	History/Social Studies	History/Social Studies	History/Social Studies
Science	Science	Science	Science	Science	Science

Week 3: Thursday, _____
(Date)

Name	Name	Name	Name	Name	Name
Math	Math	Math	Math	Math	Math
English	English	English	English	English	English
Religion	Religion	Religion	Religion	Religion	Religion
History/Social Studies	History/Social Studies	History/Social Studies	History/Social Studies	History/Social Studies	History/Social Studies
Science	Science	Science	Science	Science	Science

Week 3: Friday, _____

(Date)

Name	Name	Name	Name	Name	Name
Math	Math	Math	Math	Math	Math
English	English	English	English	English	English
Religion	Religion	Religion	Religion	Religion	Religion
History/Social Studies	History/Social Studies	History/Social Studies	History/Social Studies	History/Social Studies	History/Social Studies
Science	Science	Science	Science	Science	Science

Week 4

Memory Scripture Verse
_____
_____

Saint of the Week
_____

Patron of…
_____

I am thankful for…
_____
_____

Grocery List

_____
_____
_____
_____
_____
_____
_____
_____
_____
_____
_____
_____
_____

Meal Planning

Sunday:
_____

Monday:
_____

Tuesday:
_____

Wednesday:
_____

Thursday:
_____

Friday:
_____

Saturday:
_____

"Prayer is the place of refuge for every worry, a foundation for cheerfulness, a source of constant happiness, a protection against sadness."

St. John Chrysostom

Week 4: Monday, _____

(Date)

Name	Name	Name	Name	Name	Name
Math	Math	Math	Math	Math	Math
English	English	English	English	English	English
Religion	Religion	Religion	Religion	Religion	Religion
History/Social Studies	History/Social Studies	History/Social Studies	History/Social Studies	History/Social Studies	History/Social Studies
Science	Science	Science	Science	Science	Science

Week 4: Tuesday, _____
(Date)

Name	Name	Name	Name	Name	Name
Math	Math	Math	Math	Math	Math
English	English	English	English	English	English
Religion	Religion	Religion	Religion	Religion	Religion
History/Social Studies	History/Social Studies	History/Social Studies	History/Social Studies	History/Social Studies	History/Social Studies
Science	Science	Science	Science	Science	Science

Week 4: Wednesday, _____

(Date)

Name	Name	Name	Name	Name	Name
Math	Math	Math	Math	Math	Math
English	English	English	English	English	English
Religion	Religion	Religion	Religion	Religion	Religion
History/Social Studies	History/Social Studies	History/Social Studies	History/Social Studies	History/Social Studies	History/Social Studies
Science	Science	Science	Science	Science	Science

Week 4: Thursday, _____
(Date)

Name	Name	Name	Name	Name	Name
Math	Math	Math	Math	Math	Math
English	English	English	English	English	English
Religion	Religion	Religion	Religion	Religion	Religion
History/Social Studies	History/Social Studies	History/Social Studies	History/Social Studies	History/Social Studies	History/Social Studies
Science	Science	Science	Science	Science	Science

Week 4: Friday, _____
(Date)

Name	Name	Name	Name	Name	Name
Math	Math	Math	Math	Math	Math
English	English	English	English	English	English
Religion	Religion	Religion	Religion	Religion	Religion
History/Social Studies	History/Social Studies	History/Social Studies	History/Social Studies	History/Social Studies	History/Social Studies
Science	Science	Science	Science	Science	Science

Week 5

Memory Scripture Verse

_____

_____

_____

Saint of the Week

_____

Patron of…

_____

I am thankful for…

_____

_____

Grocery List

_____
_____
_____
_____
_____
_____
_____
_____
_____
_____
_____
_____
_____

Meal Planning

Sunday:
_____

Monday:
_____

Tuesday:
_____

Wednesday:
_____

Thursday:
_____

Friday:
_____

Saturday:
_____

"We know that in everything God works for good with those who love him, who are called according to his purpose." – Romans 8:28

Week 5: Monday, _____
(Date)

Name	Name	Name	Name	Name	Name
Math	Math	Math	Math	Math	Math
English	English	English	English	English	English
Religion	Religion	Religion	Religion	Religion	Religion
History/Social Studies	History/Social Studies	History/Social Studies	History/Social Studies	History/Social Studies	History/Social Studies
Science	Science	Science	Science	Science	Science

Week 5: Tuesday, _____
(Date)

Name	Name	Name	Name	Name	Name
Math	Math	Math	Math	Math	Math
English	English	English	English	English	English
Religion	Religion	Religion	Religion	Religion	Religion
History/Social Studies	History/Social Studies	History/Social Studies	History/Social Studies	History/Social Studies	History/Social Studies
Science	Science	Science	Science	Science	Science

Week 5: Wednesday, _____
(Date)

Name	Name	Name	Name	Name	Name
Math	Math	Math	Math	Math	Math
English	English	English	English	English	English
Religion	Religion	Religion	Religion	Religion	Religion
History/Social Studies	History/Social Studies	History/Social Studies	History/Social Studies	History/Social Studies	History/Social Studies
Science	Science	Science	Science	Science	Science

Week 5: Thursday, _____
(Date)

Name	Name	Name	Name	Name	Name
Math	Math	Math	Math	Math	Math
English	English	English	English	English	English
Religion	Religion	Religion	Religion	Religion	Religion
History/Social Studies	History/Social Studies	History/Social Studies	History/Social Studies	History/Social Studies	History/Social Studies
Science	Science	Science	Science	Science	Science

Week 5: Friday, _____

(Date)

Name	Name	Name	Name	Name	Name
Math	Math	Math	Math	Math	Math
English	English	English	English	English	English
Religion	Religion	Religion	Religion	Religion	Religion
History/Social Studies	History/Social Studies	History/Social Studies	History/Social Studies	History/Social Studies	History/Social Studies
Science	Science	Science	Science	Science	Science

Week 6

Memory Scripture Verse

_____

_____

_____

Saint of the Week

_____

Patron of…

_____

I am thankful for…

_____

_____

_____

Grocery List

_____
_____
_____
_____
_____
_____
_____
_____
_____
_____
_____
_____

Meal Planning

Sunday:
_____

Monday:
_____

Tuesday:
_____

Wednesday:
_____

Thursday:
_____

Friday:
_____

Saturday:
_____

"Patience is the companion of wisdom."
St. Augustine of Hippo

Week 6: Monday, _____
(Date)

Name	Name	Name	Name	Name	Name
Math	Math	Math	Math	Math	Math
English	English	English	English	English	English
Religion	Religion	Religion	Religion	Religion	Religion
History/Social Studies	History/Social Studies	History/Social Studies	History/Social Studies	History/Social Studies	History/Social Studies
Science	Science	Science	Science	Science	Science

Week 6: Tuesday, _____
(Date)

Name ____	Name ____	Name ____	Name ____	Name ____	Name ____
Math ____ ____ ____	Math ____ ____ ____	Math ____ ____ ____	Math ____ ____ ____	Math ____ ____ ____	Math ____ ____ ____
English ____ ____ ____	English ____ ____ ____	English ____ ____ ____	English ____ ____ ____	English ____ ____ ____	English ____ ____ ____
Religion ____ ____ ____	Religion ____ ____ ____	Religion ____ ____ ____	Religion ____ ____ ____	Religion ____ ____ ____	Religion ____ ____ ____
History/Social Studies ____ ____ ____	History/Social Studies ____ ____ ____	History/Social Studies ____ ____ ____	History/Social Studies ____ ____ ____	History/Social Studies ____ ____ ____	History/Social Studies ____ ____ ____
Science ____ ____ ____	Science ____ ____ ____	Science ____ ____ ____	Science ____ ____ ____	Science ____ ____ ____	Science ____ ____ ____
____ ____ ____ ____	____ ____ ____ ____	____ ____ ____ ____	____ ____ ____ ____	____ ____ ____ ____	____ ____ ____ ____
____ ____ ____ ____	____ ____ ____ ____	____ ____ ____ ____	____ ____ ____ ____	____ ____ ____ ____	____ ____ ____ ____
____ ____ ____ ____	____ ____ ____ ____	____ ____ ____ ____	____ ____ ____ ____	____ ____ ____ ____	____ ____ ____ ____

Week 6: Wednesday, _____

(Date)

Name	Name	Name	Name	Name	Name
Math	Math	Math	Math	Math	Math
English	English	English	English	English	English
Religion	Religion	Religion	Religion	Religion	Religion
History/Social Studies	History/Social Studies	History/Social Studies	History/Social Studies	History/Social Studies	History/Social Studies
Science	Science	Science	Science	Science	Science

Week 6: Thursday, _____

(Date)

Name	Name	Name	Name	Name	Name
Math	Math	Math	Math	Math	Math
English	English	English	English	English	English
Religion	Religion	Religion	Religion	Religion	Religion
History/Social Studies	History/Social Studies	History/Social Studies	History/Social Studies	History/Social Studies	History/Social Studies
Science	Science	Science	Science	Science	Science

Week 6: Friday, _____

(Date)

Name	Name	Name	Name	Name	Name
Math	Math	Math	Math	Math	Math
English	English	English	English	English	English
Religion	Religion	Religion	Religion	Religion	Religion
History/Social Studies	History/Social Studies	History/Social Studies	History/Social Studies	History/Social Studies	History/Social Studies
Science	Science	Science	Science	Science	Science

Week 7

Memory Scripture Verse

_____

_____

Saint of the Week

_____

Patron of…

_____

I am thankful for…

_____

_____

Grocery List

_____
_____
_____
_____
_____
_____
_____
_____
_____
_____
_____

Meal Planning

Sunday:
_____

Monday:
_____

Tuesday:
_____

Wednesday:
_____

Thursday:
_____

Friday:
_____

Saturday:
_____

"How often I failed in my duty to God because I was not leaning on the strong pillar of prayer." - St. Teresa of Avila

Week 7: Monday, _____
(Date)

Name	Name	Name	Name	Name	Name
Math	Math	Math	Math	Math	Math
English	English	English	English	English	English
Religion	Religion	Religion	Religion	Religion	Religion
History/Social Studies	History/Social Studies	History/Social Studies	History/Social Studies	History/Social Studies	History/Social Studies
Science	Science	Science	Science	Science	Science

Week 7: Tuesday, _____
(Date)

Name	Name	Name	Name	Name	Name
Math	Math	Math	Math	Math	Math
English	English	English	English	English	English
Religion	Religion	Religion	Religion	Religion	Religion
History/Social Studies	History/Social Studies	History/Social Studies	History/Social Studies	History/Social Studies	History/Social Studies
Science	Science	Science	Science	Science	Science

Week 7: Wednesday, _____

(Date)

Name	Name	Name	Name	Name	Name
Math	Math	Math	Math	Math	Math
English	English	English	English	English	English
Religion	Religion	Religion	Religion	Religion	Religion
History/Social Studies	History/Social Studies	History/Social Studies	History/Social Studies	History/Social Studies	History/Social Studies
Science	Science	Science	Science	Science	Science

Week 7: Thursday, _____
(Date)

Name	Name	Name	Name	Name	Name
Math	Math	Math	Math	Math	Math
English	English	English	English	English	English
Religion	Religion	Religion	Religion	Religion	Religion
History/Social Studies	History/Social Studies	History/Social Studies	History/Social Studies	History/Social Studies	History/Social Studies
Science	Science	Science	Science	Science	Science

Week 7: Friday, _____
(Date)

Name	Name	Name	Name	Name	Name
Math	Math	Math	Math	Math	Math
English	English	English	English	English	English
Religion	Religion	Religion	Religion	Religion	Religion
History/Social Studies	History/Social Studies	History/Social Studies	History/Social Studies	History/Social Studies	History/Social Studies
Science	Science	Science	Science	Science	Science

Week 8

Memory Scripture Verse

_____

_____

_____

Saint of the Week

_____

Patron of…

_____

I am thankful for…

_____

_____

_____

Grocery List

_____
_____
_____
_____
_____
_____
_____
_____
_____
_____
_____
_____

Meal Planning

Sunday:
_____

Monday:
_____

Tuesday:
_____

Wednesday:
_____

Thursday:
_____

Friday:
_____

Saturday:
_____

"If God is for us, who is against us?"

Romans 8:31

Week 8: Monday, _____

(Date)

Name	Name	Name	Name	Name	Name
Math	Math	Math	Math	Math	Math
English	English	English	English	English	English
Religion	Religion	Religion	Religion	Religion	Religion
History/Social Studies	History/Social Studies	History/Social Studies	History/Social Studies	History/Social Studies	History/Social Studies
Science	Science	Science	Science	Science	Science

Week 8: Tuesday, _____
(Date)

Name	Name	Name	Name	Name	Name
Math	Math	Math	Math	Math	Math
English	English	English	English	English	English
Religion	Religion	Religion	Religion	Religion	Religion
History/Social Studies	History/Social Studies	History/Social Studies	History/Social Studies	History/Social Studies	History/Social Studies
Science	Science	Science	Science	Science	Science

Week 8: Wednesday, _____

(Date)

Name	Name	Name	Name	Name	Name
Math	Math	Math	Math	Math	Math
English	English	English	English	English	English
Religion	Religion	Religion	Religion	Religion	Religion
History/Social Studies	History/Social Studies	History/Social Studies	History/Social Studies	History/Social Studies	History/Social Studies
Science	Science	Science	Science	Science	Science

Week 8: Thursday, _____
(Date)

Name	Name	Name	Name	Name	Name
Math	Math	Math	Math	Math	Math
English	English	English	English	English	English
Religion	Religion	Religion	Religion	Religion	Religion
History/Social Studies	History/Social Studies	History/Social Studies	History/Social Studies	History/Social Studies	History/Social Studies
Science	Science	Science	Science	Science	Science

Week 8: Friday, _____
(Date)

Name	Name	Name	Name	Name	Name
Math	Math	Math	Math	Math	Math
English	English	English	English	English	English
Religion	Religion	Religion	Religion	Religion	Religion
History/Social Studies	History/Social Studies	History/Social Studies	History/Social Studies	History/Social Studies	History/Social Studies
Science	Science	Science	Science	Science	Science

Week 9

Memory Scripture Verse
_____
_____
_____

Saint of the Week
_____

Patron of…
_____

I am thankful for…
_____
_____
_____

Grocery List

_____
_____
_____
_____
_____
_____
_____
_____
_____
_____
_____
_____
_____

Meal Planning

Sunday:
_____

Monday:
_____

Tuesday:
_____

Wednesday:
_____

Thursday:
_____

Friday:
_____

Saturday:
_____

"Don't get upset with your imperfections…. Simply surrender to the Power of God's Love, which is always greater than our weakness."

St. Francis De Sales

Week 9: Monday, _____
(Date)

Name	Name	Name	Name	Name	Name
Math	Math	Math	Math	Math	Math
English	English	English	English	English	English
Religion	Religion	Religion	Religion	Religion	Religion
History/Social Studies	History/Social Studies	History/Social Studies	History/Social Studies	History/Social Studies	History/Social Studies
Science	Science	Science	Science	Science	Science

Week 9: Tuesday, _____

(Date)

Name	Name	Name	Name	Name	Name
Math	Math	Math	Math	Math	Math
English	English	English	English	English	English
Religion	Religion	Religion	Religion	Religion	Religion
History/Social Studies	History/Social Studies	History/Social Studies	History/Social Studies	History/Social Studies	History/Social Studies
Science	Science	Science	Science	Science	Science

Week 9: Wednesday, _____

(Date)

Name	Name	Name	Name	Name	Name
Math	Math	Math	Math	Math	Math
English	English	English	English	English	English
Religion	Religion	Religion	Religion	Religion	Religion
History/Social Studies	History/Social Studies	History/Social Studies	History/Social Studies	History/Social Studies	History/Social Studies
Science	Science	Science	Science	Science	Science

Week 9: Thursday, _____
(Date)

Name	Name	Name	Name	Name	Name
Math	Math	Math	Math	Math	Math
English	English	English	English	English	English
Religion	Religion	Religion	Religion	Religion	Religion
History/Social Studies	History/Social Studies	History/Social Studies	History/Social Studies	History/Social Studies	History/Social Studies
Science	Science	Science	Science	Science	Science

Week 9: Friday, _____
(Date)

Name	Name	Name	Name	Name	Name
Math	Math	Math	Math	Math	Math
English	English	English	English	English	English
Religion	Religion	Religion	Religion	Religion	Religion
History/Social Studies	History/Social Studies	History/Social Studies	History/Social Studies	History/Social Studies	History/Social Studies
Science	Science	Science	Science	Science	Science

Week 10

Memory Scripture Verse

_____

_____

_____

Saint of the Week

_____

Patron of…

_____

I am thankful for…

_____

_____

Grocery List

_____
_____
_____
_____
_____
_____
_____
_____
_____
_____
_____
_____
_____

Meal Planning

Sunday:
_____

Monday:
_____

Tuesday:
_____

Wednesday:
_____

Thursday:
_____

Friday:
_____

Saturday:
_____

"Begin now… believe me, don't wait until tomorrow to begin becoming a saint."

St. Thérèse of Lisieux

Week 10: Monday, _____
(Date)

Name	Name	Name	Name	Name	Name
Math	Math	Math	Math	Math	Math
English	English	English	English	English	English
Religion	Religion	Religion	Religion	Religion	Religion
History/Social Studies	History/Social Studies	History/Social Studies	History/Social Studies	History/Social Studies	History/Social Studies
Science	Science	Science	Science	Science	Science

Week 10: Tuesday, _____
(Date)

Name	Name	Name	Name	Name	Name
Math	Math	Math	Math	Math	Math
English	English	English	English	English	English
Religion	Religion	Religion	Religion	Religion	Religion
History/Social Studies	History/Social Studies	History/Social Studies	History/Social Studies	History/Social Studies	History/Social Studies
Science	Science	Science	Science	Science	Science

Week 10: Wednesday, _____
(Date)

Name	Name	Name	Name	Name	Name
Math	Math	Math	Math	Math	Math
English	English	English	English	English	English
Religion	Religion	Religion	Religion	Religion	Religion
History/Social Studies	History/Social Studies	History/Social Studies	History/Social Studies	History/Social Studies	History/Social Studies
Science	Science	Science	Science	Science	Science

Week 10: Thursday, _____

(Date)

Name	Name	Name	Name	Name	Name
Math	Math	Math	Math	Math	Math
English	English	English	English	English	English
Religion	Religion	Religion	Religion	Religion	Religion
History/Social Studies	History/Social Studies	History/Social Studies	History/Social Studies	History/Social Studies	History/Social Studies
Science	Science	Science	Science	Science	Science

Week 10: Friday, _____

(Date)

Name	Name	Name	Name	Name	Name
Math	Math	Math	Math	Math	Math
English	English	English	English	English	English
Religion	Religion	Religion	Religion	Religion	Religion
History/Social Studies	History/Social Studies	History/Social Studies	History/Social Studies	History/Social Studies	History/Social Studies
Science	Science	Science	Science	Science	Science

Week 11

Memory Scripture Verse

Saint of the Week

I am thankful for…

Patron of…

Grocery List

Meal Planning

Sunday:

Monday:

Tuesday:

Wednesday:

Thursday:

Friday:

Saturday:

"God loves each of us as if there were only one of us."
Saint Augustine of Hippo

Week 11: Monday, _____
(Date)

Name	Name	Name	Name	Name	Name
Math	Math	Math	Math	Math	Math
English	English	English	English	English	English
Religion	Religion	Religion	Religion	Religion	Religion
History/Social Studies	History/Social Studies	History/Social Studies	History/Social Studies	History/Social Studies	History/Social Studies
Science	Science	Science	Science	Science	Science

Week 11: Tuesday, _____

(Date)

Name	Name	Name	Name	Name	Name
Math	Math	Math	Math	Math	Math
English	English	English	English	English	English
Religion	Religion	Religion	Religion	Religion	Religion
History/Social Studies	History/Social Studies	History/Social Studies	History/Social Studies	History/Social Studies	History/Social Studies
Science	Science	Science	Science	Science	Science

Week 11: Wednesday, _____
(Date)

Name	Name	Name	Name	Name	Name
Math	Math	Math	Math	Math	Math
English	English	English	English	English	English
Religion	Religion	Religion	Religion	Religion	Religion
History/Social Studies	History/Social Studies	History/Social Studies	History/Social Studies	History/Social Studies	History/Social Studies
Science	Science	Science	Science	Science	Science

Week 11: Thursday, _____

(Date)

Name	Name	Name	Name	Name	Name
Math	Math	Math	Math	Math	Math
English	English	English	English	English	English
Religion	Religion	Religion	Religion	Religion	Religion
History/Social Studies	History/Social Studies	History/Social Studies	History/Social Studies	History/Social Studies	History/Social Studies
Science	Science	Science	Science	Science	Science

Week 11: Friday, _____
(Date)

Name	Name	Name	Name	Name	Name
Math	Math	Math	Math	Math	Math
English	English	English	English	English	English
Religion	Religion	Religion	Religion	Religion	Religion
History/Social Studies	History/Social Studies	History/Social Studies	History/Social Studies	History/Social Studies	History/Social Studies
Science	Science	Science	Science	Science	Science

Week 12

Memory Scripture Verse

_____

_____

_____

Saint of the Week

_____

Patron of…

_____

I am thankful for…

_____

_____

Grocery List

_____
_____
_____
_____
_____
_____
_____
_____
_____
_____
_____
_____
_____

Meal Planning

Sunday:
_____

Monday:
_____

Tuesday:
_____

Wednesday:
_____

Thursday:
_____

Friday:
_____

Saturday:
_____

"Do not be anxious about your life, what you shall eat or what you shall drink, nor about your body, what you shall put on. Is not life more than food, and the body more than clothing?" – Matthew 6:25

Week 12: Monday, _____

(Date)

Name	Name	Name	Name	Name	Name
Math	Math	Math	Math	Math	Math
English	English	English	English	English	English
Religion	Religion	Religion	Religion	Religion	Religion
History/Social Studies	History/Social Studies	History/Social Studies	History/Social Studies	History/Social Studies	History/Social Studies
Science	Science	Science	Science	Science	Science

Week 12: Tuesday, _____
(Date)

Name	Name	Name	Name	Name	Name
Math	Math	Math	Math	Math	Math
English	English	English	English	English	English
Religion	Religion	Religion	Religion	Religion	Religion
History/Social Studies	History/Social Studies	History/Social Studies	History/Social Studies	History/Social Studies	History/Social Studies
Science	Science	Science	Science	Science	Science

Week 12: Wednesday, _____

(Date)

Name	Name	Name	Name	Name	Name
Math	Math	Math	Math	Math	Math
English	English	English	English	English	English
Religion	Religion	Religion	Religion	Religion	Religion
History/Social Studies	History/Social Studies	History/Social Studies	History/Social Studies	History/Social Studies	History/Social Studies
Science	Science	Science	Science	Science	Science

Week 12: Thursday, _____

(Date)

Name	Name	Name	Name	Name	Name
Math	Math	Math	Math	Math	Math
English	English	English	English	English	English
Religion	Religion	Religion	Religion	Religion	Religion
History/Social Studies	History/Social Studies	History/Social Studies	History/Social Studies	History/Social Studies	History/Social Studies
Science	Science	Science	Science	Science	Science

Week 12: Friday, _____
(Date)

Name	Name	Name	Name	Name	Name
Math	Math	Math	Math	Math	Math
English	English	English	English	English	English
Religion	Religion	Religion	Religion	Religion	Religion
History/Social Studies	History/Social Studies	History/Social Studies	History/Social Studies	History/Social Studies	History/Social Studies
Science	Science	Science	Science	Science	Science

Week 13

Memory Scripture Verse

_____

_____

_____

Saint of the Week

_____

Patron of…

_____

I am thankful for…

_____

_____

Grocery List

_____
_____
_____
_____
_____
_____
_____
_____
_____
_____
_____
_____

Meal Planning

Sunday:
_____

Monday:
_____

Tuesday:
_____

Wednesday:
_____

Thursday:
_____

Friday:
_____

Saturday:
_____

"While the world changes, the cross stands firm."

St. Bruno

Week 13: Monday, _____
(Date)

Name	Name	Name	Name	Name	Name
Math	Math	Math	Math	Math	Math
English	English	English	English	English	English
Religion	Religion	Religion	Religion	Religion	Religion
History/Social Studies	History/Social Studies	History/Social Studies	History/Social Studies	History/Social Studies	History/Social Studies
Science	Science	Science	Science	Science	Science

Week 13: Tuesday, _____
(Date)

Name	Name	Name	Name	Name	Name
Math	Math	Math	Math	Math	Math
English	English	English	English	English	English
Religion	Religion	Religion	Religion	Religion	Religion
History/Social Studies	History/Social Studies	History/Social Studies	History/Social Studies	History/Social Studies	History/Social Studies
Science	Science	Science	Science	Science	Science

Week 13: Wednesday, _____

(Date)

Name	Name	Name	Name	Name	Name
Math	Math	Math	Math	Math	Math
English	English	English	English	English	English
Religion	Religion	Religion	Religion	Religion	Religion
History/Social Studies	History/Social Studies	History/Social Studies	History/Social Studies	History/Social Studies	History/Social Studies
Science	Science	Science	Science	Science	Science

Week 13: Thursday, _____
(Date)

Name	Name	Name	Name	Name	Name
Math	Math	Math	Math	Math	Math
English	English	English	English	English	English
Religion	Religion	Religion	Religion	Religion	Religion
History/Social Studies	History/Social Studies	History/Social Studies	History/Social Studies	History/Social Studies	History/Social Studies
Science	Science	Science	Science	Science	Science

Week 13: Friday, _____

(Date)

Name	Name	Name	Name	Name	Name
Math	Math	Math	Math	Math	Math
English	English	English	English	English	English
Religion	Religion	Religion	Religion	Religion	Religion
History/Social Studies	History/Social Studies	History/Social Studies	History/Social Studies	History/Social Studies	History/Social Studies
Science	Science	Science	Science	Science	Science

Week 14

Memory Scripture Verse

_____

_____

_____

Saint of the Week

_____

Patron of…

_____

I am thankful for…

_____

_____

_____

Grocery List

_____
_____
_____
_____
_____
_____
_____
_____
_____
_____
_____
_____
_____
_____

Meal Planning

Sunday:
_____

Monday:
_____

Tuesday:
_____

Wednesday:
_____

Thursday:
_____

Friday:
_____

Saturday:
_____

"To maintain a joyful family requires much from both the parents and the children. Each member of the family has to become, in a special way, the servant of the others." - St. John Paul II

Week 14: Monday, _____

(Date)

Name	Name	Name	Name	Name	Name
Math	Math	Math	Math	Math	Math
English	English	English	English	English	English
Religion	Religion	Religion	Religion	Religion	Religion
History/Social Studies	History/Social Studies	History/Social Studies	History/Social Studies	History/Social Studies	History/Social Studies
Science	Science	Science	Science	Science	Science

Week 14: Tuesday, _____
(Date)

Name	Name	Name	Name	Name	Name
Math	Math	Math	Math	Math	Math
English	English	English	English	English	English
Religion	Religion	Religion	Religion	Religion	Religion
History/Social Studies	History/Social Studies	History/Social Studies	History/Social Studies	History/Social Studies	History/Social Studies
Science	Science	Science	Science	Science	Science

Week 14: Wednesday, _____

(Date)

Name	Name	Name	Name	Name	Name
Math	Math	Math	Math	Math	Math
English	English	English	English	English	English
Religion	Religion	Religion	Religion	Religion	Religion
History/Social Studies	History/Social Studies	History/Social Studies	History/Social Studies	History/Social Studies	History/Social Studies
Science	Science	Science	Science	Science	Science

Week 14: Thursday, _____

(Date)

Name	Name	Name	Name	Name	Name
Math	Math	Math	Math	Math	Math
English	English	English	English	English	English
Religion	Religion	Religion	Religion	Religion	Religion
History/Social Studies	History/Social Studies	History/Social Studies	History/Social Studies	History/Social Studies	History/Social Studies
Science	Science	Science	Science	Science	Science

Week 14: Friday, _____

(Date)

Name	Name	Name	Name	Name	Name
Math	Math	Math	Math	Math	Math
English	English	English	English	English	English
Religion	Religion	Religion	Religion	Religion	Religion
History/Social Studies	History/Social Studies	History/Social Studies	History/Social Studies	History/Social Studies	History/Social Studies
Science	Science	Science	Science	Science	Science

Week 15

Memory Scripture Verse

Saint of the Week

I am thankful for…

Patron of…

Grocery List

Meal Planning

Sunday:

Monday:

Tuesday:

Wednesday:

Thursday:

Friday:

Saturday:

"Keep your heart in peace and let nothing trouble you, not even your faults… for God's dwelling is in peace." - St. Margaret Mary Alacoque

Week 15: Monday, _____
(Date)

Name	Name	Name	Name	Name	Name
Math	Math	Math	Math	Math	Math
English	English	English	English	English	English
Religion	Religion	Religion	Religion	Religion	Religion
History/Social Studies	History/Social Studies	History/Social Studies	History/Social Studies	History/Social Studies	History/Social Studies
Science	Science	Science	Science	Science	Science

Week 15: Tuesday, _____
(Date)

Name	Name	Name	Name	Name	Name
Math	Math	Math	Math	Math	Math
English	English	English	English	English	English
Religion	Religion	Religion	Religion	Religion	Religion
History/Social Studies	History/Social Studies	History/Social Studies	History/Social Studies	History/Social Studies	History/Social Studies
Science	Science	Science	Science	Science	Science

Week 15: Wednesday, _____

(Date)

Name	Name	Name	Name	Name	Name
Math	Math	Math	Math	Math	Math
English	English	English	English	English	English
Religion	Religion	Religion	Religion	Religion	Religion
History/Social Studies	History/Social Studies	History/Social Studies	History/Social Studies	History/Social Studies	History/Social Studies
Science	Science	Science	Science	Science	Science

Week 15: Thursday, _____
(Date)

Name	Name	Name	Name	Name	Name
Math	Math	Math	Math	Math	Math
English	English	English	English	English	English
Religion	Religion	Religion	Religion	Religion	Religion
History/Social Studies	History/Social Studies	History/Social Studies	History/Social Studies	History/Social Studies	History/Social Studies
Science	Science	Science	Science	Science	Science

Week 15: Friday, _____
(Date)

Name	Name	Name	Name	Name	Name
Math	Math	Math	Math	Math	Math
English	English	English	English	English	English
Religion	Religion	Religion	Religion	Religion	Religion
History/Social Studies	History/Social Studies	History/Social Studies	History/Social Studies	History/Social Studies	History/Social Studies
Science	Science	Science	Science	Science	Science

Week 16

Memory Scripture Verse

_____

_____

_____

Saint of the Week

_____

Patron of…

_____

I am thankful for…

_____

_____

_____

Grocery List

_____
_____
_____
_____
_____
_____
_____
_____
_____
_____
_____
_____
_____
_____

Meal Planning

Sunday:
_____

Monday:
_____

Tuesday:
_____

Wednesday:
_____

Thursday:
_____

Friday:
_____

Saturday:
_____

"Our Lord has created persons for all states in life, and in all of them we see people who achieved sanctity by fulfilling their obligations well."

St. Anthony Mary Claret

Week 16: Monday, _____
(Date)

Name ___	Name ___	Name ___	Name ___	Name ___	Name ___
Math	Math	Math	Math	Math	Math
English	English	English	English	English	English
Religion	Religion	Religion	Religion	Religion	Religion
History/Social Studies	History/Social Studies	History/Social Studies	History/Social Studies	History/Social Studies	History/Social Studies
Science	Science	Science	Science	Science	Science

Week 16: Tuesday, _____

(Date)

Name	Name	Name	Name	Name	Name
Math	Math	Math	Math	Math	Math
English	English	English	English	English	English
Religion	Religion	Religion	Religion	Religion	Religion
History/Social Studies	History/Social Studies	History/Social Studies	History/Social Studies	History/Social Studies	History/Social Studies
Science	Science	Science	Science	Science	Science

Week 16: Wednesday, _____

(Date)

Name	Name	Name	Name	Name	Name
Math	Math	Math	Math	Math	Math
English	English	English	English	English	English
Religion	Religion	Religion	Religion	Religion	Religion
History/Social Studies	History/Social Studies	History/Social Studies	History/Social Studies	History/Social Studies	History/Social Studies
Science	Science	Science	Science	Science	Science

Week 16: Thursday, _____

(Date)

Name	Name	Name	Name	Name	Name
Math	Math	Math	Math	Math	Math
English	English	English	English	English	English
Religion	Religion	Religion	Religion	Religion	Religion
History/Social Studies	History/Social Studies	History/Social Studies	History/Social Studies	History/Social Studies	History/Social Studies
Science	Science	Science	Science	Science	Science

Week 16: Friday, _____

(Date)

Name	Name	Name	Name	Name	Name
Math	Math	Math	Math	Math	Math
English	English	English	English	English	English
Religion	Religion	Religion	Religion	Religion	Religion
History/Social Studies	History/Social Studies	History/Social Studies	History/Social Studies	History/Social Studies	History/Social Studies
Science	Science	Science	Science	Science	Science

Week 17

Memory Scripture Verse

_____

_____

_____

Saint of the Week

_____

Patron of…

_____

I am thankful for…

_____

_____

_____

Grocery List

_____
_____
_____
_____
_____
_____
_____
_____
_____
_____
_____
_____

Meal Planning

Sunday:
_____

Monday:
_____

Tuesday:
_____

Wednesday:
_____

Thursday:
_____

Friday:
_____

Saturday:
_____

"The first end I propose in our daily work is to do the will of God; secondly, to do it in the manner He wills it; and thirdly to do it because it is His will."

St. Elizabeth Ann Seton

Week 17: Monday, _____
(Date)

Name	Name	Name	Name	Name	Name
Math	Math	Math	Math	Math	Math
English	English	English	English	English	English
Religion	Religion	Religion	Religion	Religion	Religion
History/Social Studies	History/Social Studies	History/Social Studies	History/Social Studies	History/Social Studies	History/Social Studies
Science	Science	Science	Science	Science	Science

Week 17: Tuesday, _____

(Date)

Name	Name	Name	Name	Name	Name
Math	Math	Math	Math	Math	Math
English	English	English	English	English	English
Religion	Religion	Religion	Religion	Religion	Religion
History/Social Studies	History/Social Studies	History/Social Studies	History/Social Studies	History/Social Studies	History/Social Studies
Science	Science	Science	Science	Science	Science

Week 17: Wednesday, _____

(Date)

Name	Name	Name	Name	Name	Name
Math	Math	Math	Math	Math	Math
English	English	English	English	English	English
Religion	Religion	Religion	Religion	Religion	Religion
History/Social Studies	History/Social Studies	History/Social Studies	History/Social Studies	History/Social Studies	History/Social Studies
Science	Science	Science	Science	Science	Science

Week 17: Thursday, _____
(Date)

Name	Name	Name	Name	Name	Name
Math	Math	Math	Math	Math	Math
English	English	English	English	English	English
Religion	Religion	Religion	Religion	Religion	Religion
History/Social Studies	History/Social Studies	History/Social Studies	History/Social Studies	History/Social Studies	History/Social Studies
Science	Science	Science	Science	Science	Science

Week 17: Friday, _____

(Date)

Name	Name	Name	Name	Name	Name
Math	Math	Math	Math	Math	Math
English	English	English	English	English	English
Religion	Religion	Religion	Religion	Religion	Religion
History/Social Studies	History/Social Studies	History/Social Studies	History/Social Studies	History/Social Studies	History/Social Studies
Science	Science	Science	Science	Science	Science

Week 18

Memory Scripture Verse

Saint of the Week

I am thankful for...

Patron of...

Grocery List

Meal Planning

Sunday:

Monday:

Tuesday:

Wednesday:

Thursday:

Friday:

Saturday:

"Joy, with peace, is the sister of charity. Serve the Lord with laughter."
St. Padre Pio

Week 18: Monday, _____
(Date)

Name	Name	Name	Name	Name	Name
Math	Math	Math	Math	Math	Math
English	English	English	English	English	English
Religion	Religion	Religion	Religion	Religion	Religion
History/Social Studies	History/Social Studies	History/Social Studies	History/Social Studies	History/Social Studies	History/Social Studies
Science	Science	Science	Science	Science	Science

Week 18: Tuesday, _____

(Date)

Name	Name	Name	Name	Name	Name
Math	Math	Math	Math	Math	Math
English	English	English	English	English	English
Religion	Religion	Religion	Religion	Religion	Religion
History/Social Studies	History/Social Studies	History/Social Studies	History/Social Studies	History/Social Studies	History/Social Studies
Science	Science	Science	Science	Science	Science

Week 18: Wednesday, _____

(Date)

Name	Name	Name	Name	Name	Name
Math	Math	Math	Math	Math	Math
English	English	English	English	English	English
Religion	Religion	Religion	Religion	Religion	Religion
History/Social Studies	History/Social Studies	History/Social Studies	History/Social Studies	History/Social Studies	History/Social Studies
Science	Science	Science	Science	Science	Science

Week 18: Thursday, _____

(Date)

Name	**Name**	**Name**	**Name**	**Name**	**Name**
Math	Math	Math	Math	Math	Math
English	English	English	English	English	English
Religion	Religion	Religion	Religion	Religion	Religion
History/Social Studies	History/Social Studies	History/Social Studies	History/Social Studies	History/Social Studies	History/Social Studies
Science	Science	Science	Science	Science	Science

Week 18: Friday, _____
(Date)

Name	Name	Name	Name	Name	Name
Math	Math	Math	Math	Math	Math
English	English	English	English	English	English
Religion	Religion	Religion	Religion	Religion	Religion
History/Social Studies	History/Social Studies	History/Social Studies	History/Social Studies	History/Social Studies	History/Social Studies
Science	Science	Science	Science	Science	Science

Week 19

Memory Scripture Verse

Saint of the Week

I am thankful for…

Patron of…

Grocery List

Meal Planning

Sunday:

Monday:

Tuesday:

Wednesday:

Thursday:

Friday:

Saturday:

"By the anxieties and worries of this life Satan tries to dull man's heart and make a dwelling for himself there." - St. Francis of Assisi

Week 19: Monday, _____
(Date)

Name	Name	Name	Name	Name	Name
Math	Math	Math	Math	Math	Math
English	English	English	English	English	English
Religion	Religion	Religion	Religion	Religion	Religion
History/Social Studies	History/Social Studies	History/Social Studies	History/Social Studies	History/Social Studies	History/Social Studies
Science	Science	Science	Science	Science	Science

Week 19: Tuesday, _____
(Date)

Name	Name	Name	Name	Name	Name
Math	Math	Math	Math	Math	Math
English	English	English	English	English	English
Religion	Religion	Religion	Religion	Religion	Religion
History/Social Studies	History/Social Studies	History/Social Studies	History/Social Studies	History/Social Studies	History/Social Studies
Science	Science	Science	Science	Science	Science

Week 19: Wednesday, _____

(Date)

Name	Name	Name	Name	Name	Name
Math	Math	Math	Math	Math	Math
English	English	English	English	English	English
Religion	Religion	Religion	Religion	Religion	Religion
History/Social Studies	History/Social Studies	History/Social Studies	History/Social Studies	History/Social Studies	History/Social Studies
Science	Science	Science	Science	Science	Science

Week 19: Thursday, _____

(Date)

Name	Name	Name	Name	Name	Name
Math	Math	Math	Math	Math	Math
English	English	English	English	English	English
Religion	Religion	Religion	Religion	Religion	Religion
History/Social Studies	History/Social Studies	History/Social Studies	History/Social Studies	History/Social Studies	History/Social Studies
Science	Science	Science	Science	Science	Science

Week 19: Friday, _____

(Date)

Name	Name	Name	Name	Name	Name
Math	Math	Math	Math	Math	Math
English	English	English	English	English	English
Religion	Religion	Religion	Religion	Religion	Religion
History/Social Studies	History/Social Studies	History/Social Studies	History/Social Studies	History/Social Studies	History/Social Studies
Science	Science	Science	Science	Science	Science

Week 20

Memory Scripture Verse
_____
_____
_____

Saint of the Week
_____

Patron of...
_____

I am thankful for...
_____
_____
_____

Grocery List

_____
_____
_____
_____
_____
_____
_____
_____
_____
_____
_____
_____
_____
_____

Meal Planning

Sunday:
_____

Monday:
_____

Tuesday:
_____

Wednesday:
_____

Thursday:
_____

Friday:
_____

Saturday:
_____

"Maintain a spirit of peace and you will save a thousand souls."
St. Seraphim of Sarov

Week 20: Monday, _____
(Date)

Name	Name	Name	Name	Name	Name
Math	Math	Math	Math	Math	Math
English	English	English	English	English	English
Religion	Religion	Religion	Religion	Religion	Religion
History/Social Studies	History/Social Studies	History/Social Studies	History/Social Studies	History/Social Studies	History/Social Studies
Science	Science	Science	Science	Science	Science

Week 20: Tuesday, _____

(Date)

Name	Name	Name	Name	Name	Name
Math	Math	Math	Math	Math	Math
English	English	English	English	English	English
Religion	Religion	Religion	Religion	Religion	Religion
History/Social Studies	History/Social Studies	History/Social Studies	History/Social Studies	History/Social Studies	History/Social Studies
Science	Science	Science	Science	Science	Science

Week 20: Wednesday, _____
(Date)

Name	Name	Name	Name	Name	Name
Math	Math	Math	Math	Math	Math
English	English	English	English	English	English
Religion	Religion	Religion	Religion	Religion	Religion
History/Social Studies	History/Social Studies	History/Social Studies	History/Social Studies	History/Social Studies	History/Social Studies
Science	Science	Science	Science	Science	Science

Week 20: Thursday, _____

(Date)

Name	Name	Name	Name	Name	Name
Math	Math	Math	Math	Math	Math
English	English	English	English	English	English
Religion	Religion	Religion	Religion	Religion	Religion
History/Social Studies	History/Social Studies	History/Social Studies	History/Social Studies	History/Social Studies	History/Social Studies
Science	Science	Science	Science	Science	Science

Week 20: Friday, _____

(Date)

Name	Name	Name	Name	Name	Name
Math	Math	Math	Math	Math	Math
English	English	English	English	English	English
Religion	Religion	Religion	Religion	Religion	Religion
History/Social Studies	History/Social Studies	History/Social Studies	History/Social Studies	History/Social Studies	History/Social Studies
Science	Science	Science	Science	Science	Science

Week 21

Memory Scripture Verse

_____

_____

_____

Saint of the Week

_____

Patron of…

_____

I am thankful for…

_____

_____

_____

Grocery List

_____
_____
_____
_____
_____
_____
_____
_____
_____
_____
_____
_____

Meal Planning

Sunday:
_____

Monday:
_____

Tuesday:
_____

Wednesday:
_____

Thursday:
_____

Friday:
_____

Saturday:
_____

"Love ought to consist of deeds more than of words."

St. Ignatius of Loyola

Week 21: Monday, _____
(Date)

Name	Name	Name	Name	Name	Name
Math	Math	Math	Math	Math	Math
English	English	English	English	English	English
Religion	Religion	Religion	Religion	Religion	Religion
History/Social Studies	History/Social Studies	History/Social Studies	History/Social Studies	History/Social Studies	History/Social Studies
Science	Science	Science	Science	Science	Science

Week 21: Tuesday, _____

(Date)

Name	Name	Name	Name	Name	Name
Math	Math	Math	Math	Math	Math
English	English	English	English	English	English
Religion	Religion	Religion	Religion	Religion	Religion
History/Social Studies	History/Social Studies	History/Social Studies	History/Social Studies	History/Social Studies	History/Social Studies
Science	Science	Science	Science	Science	Science

Week 21: Wednesday, _____

(Date)

Name	Name	Name	Name	Name	Name
Math	Math	Math	Math	Math	Math
English	English	English	English	English	English
Religion	Religion	Religion	Religion	Religion	Religion
History/Social Studies	History/Social Studies	History/Social Studies	History/Social Studies	History/Social Studies	History/Social Studies
Science	Science	Science	Science	Science	Science

Week 21: Thursday, _____

(Date)

Name	Name	Name	Name	Name	Name
Math	Math	Math	Math	Math	Math
English	English	English	English	English	English
Religion	Religion	Religion	Religion	Religion	Religion
History/Social Studies	History/Social Studies	History/Social Studies	History/Social Studies	History/Social Studies	History/Social Studies
Science	Science	Science	Science	Science	Science

Week 21: Friday, _____

(Date)

Name	Name	Name	Name	Name	Name
Math	Math	Math	Math	Math	Math
English	English	English	English	English	English
Religion	Religion	Religion	Religion	Religion	Religion
History/Social Studies	History/Social Studies	History/Social Studies	History/Social Studies	History/Social Studies	History/Social Studies
Science	Science	Science	Science	Science	Science

Week 22

Memory Scripture Verse
_____
_____
_____

Saint of the Week
_____

Patron of...
_____

I am thankful for...
_____
_____
_____

Grocery List

_____
_____
_____
_____
_____
_____
_____
_____
_____
_____
_____
_____
_____

Meal Planning

Sunday:
_____

Monday:
_____

Tuesday:
_____

Wednesday:
_____

Thursday:
_____

Friday:
_____

Saturday:
_____

"Do not worry over things that generate preoccupation and anxiety. One thing only is necessary: to lift up your spirit and love to God."
St. Padre Pio

Week 22: Monday, _____

(Date)

Name	Name	Name	Name	Name	Name
Math	Math	Math	Math	Math	Math
English	English	English	English	English	English
Religion	Religion	Religion	Religion	Religion	Religion
History/Social Studies	History/Social Studies	History/Social Studies	History/Social Studies	History/Social Studies	History/Social Studies
Science	Science	Science	Science	Science	Science

Week 22: Tuesday, _____
(Date)

Name	Name	Name	Name	Name	Name
Math	Math	Math	Math	Math	Math
English	English	English	English	English	English
Religion	Religion	Religion	Religion	Religion	Religion
History/Social Studies	History/Social Studies	History/Social Studies	History/Social Studies	History/Social Studies	History/Social Studies
Science	Science	Science	Science	Science	Science

Week 22: Wednesday, _____
(Date)

Name	Name	Name	Name	Name	Name
Math	Math	Math	Math	Math	Math
English	English	English	English	English	English
Religion	Religion	Religion	Religion	Religion	Religion
History/Social Studies	History/Social Studies	History/Social Studies	History/Social Studies	History/Social Studies	History/Social Studies
Science	Science	Science	Science	Science	Science

Week 22: Thursday, _____
(Date)

Name	Name	Name	Name	Name	Name
Math	Math	Math	Math	Math	Math
English	English	English	English	English	English
Religion	Religion	Religion	Religion	Religion	Religion
History/Social Studies	History/Social Studies	History/Social Studies	History/Social Studies	History/Social Studies	History/Social Studies
Science	Science	Science	Science	Science	Science

Week 22: Friday, _____
(Date)

Name	Name	Name	Name	Name	Name
Math	Math	Math	Math	Math	Math
English	English	English	English	English	English
Religion	Religion	Religion	Religion	Religion	Religion
History/Social Studies	History/Social Studies	History/Social Studies	History/Social Studies	History/Social Studies	History/Social Studies
Science	Science	Science	Science	Science	Science

Week 23

Memory Scripture Verse

Saint of the Week

I am thankful for…

Patron of…

Grocery List

Meal Planning

Sunday:

Monday:

Tuesday:

Wednesday:

Thursday:

Friday:

Saturday:

"If you are what you should be, you will set the whole world ablaze!"
Saint Catherine of Siena

Week 23: Monday, _____
(Date)

Name	Name	Name	Name	Name	Name
Math	Math	Math	Math	Math	Math
English	English	English	English	English	English
Religion	Religion	Religion	Religion	Religion	Religion
History/Social Studies	History/Social Studies	History/Social Studies	History/Social Studies	History/Social Studies	History/Social Studies
Science	Science	Science	Science	Science	Science

Week 23: Tuesday, _____

(Date)

Name	Name	Name	Name	Name	Name
Math	Math	Math	Math	Math	Math
English	English	English	English	English	English
Religion	Religion	Religion	Religion	Religion	Religion
History/Social Studies	History/Social Studies	History/Social Studies	History/Social Studies	History/Social Studies	History/Social Studies
Science	Science	Science	Science	Science	Science

Week 23: Wednesday, _____

(Date)

Name	Name	Name	Name	Name	Name
Math	Math	Math	Math	Math	Math
English	English	English	English	English	English
Religion	Religion	Religion	Religion	Religion	Religion
History/Social Studies	History/Social Studies	History/Social Studies	History/Social Studies	History/Social Studies	History/Social Studies
Science	Science	Science	Science	Science	Science

Week 23: Thursday, _____

(Date)

Name	Name	Name	Name	Name	Name
Math	Math	Math	Math	Math	Math
English	English	English	English	English	English
Religion	Religion	Religion	Religion	Religion	Religion
History/Social Studies	History/Social Studies	History/Social Studies	History/Social Studies	History/Social Studies	History/Social Studies
Science	Science	Science	Science	Science	Science

Week 23: Friday, _____
(Date)

Name	Name	Name	Name	Name	Name
Math	Math	Math	Math	Math	Math
English	English	English	English	English	English
Religion	Religion	Religion	Religion	Religion	Religion
History/Social Studies	History/Social Studies	History/Social Studies	History/Social Studies	History/Social Studies	History/Social Studies
Science	Science	Science	Science	Science	Science

Week 24

Memory Scripture Verse

Saint of the Week

I am thankful for…

Patron of…

Grocery List

Meal Planning

Sunday:

Monday:

Tuesday:

Wednesday:

Thursday:

Friday:

Saturday:

"Jesus, help me to simplify my life by learning what you want me to be and becoming that person."

Saint Thérèse of Lisieux

Week 24: Monday, _____
(Date)

Name	Name	Name	Name	Name	Name
Math	Math	Math	Math	Math	Math
English	English	English	English	English	English
Religion	Religion	Religion	Religion	Religion	Religion
History/Social Studies	History/Social Studies	History/Social Studies	History/Social Studies	History/Social Studies	History/Social Studies
Science	Science	Science	Science	Science	Science

Week 24: Tuesday, _____

(Date)

Name	Name	Name	Name	Name	Name
Math	Math	Math	Math	Math	Math
English	English	English	English	English	English
Religion	Religion	Religion	Religion	Religion	Religion
History/Social Studies	History/Social Studies	History/Social Studies	History/Social Studies	History/Social Studies	History/Social Studies
Science	Science	Science	Science	Science	Science

Week 24: Wednesday, _____

(Date)

Name	Name	Name	Name	Name	Name
Math	Math	Math	Math	Math	Math
English	English	English	English	English	English
Religion	Religion	Religion	Religion	Religion	Religion
History/Social Studies	History/Social Studies	History/Social Studies	History/Social Studies	History/Social Studies	History/Social Studies
Science	Science	Science	Science	Science	Science

Week 24: Thursday, _____

(Date)

Name	Name	Name	Name	Name	Name
Math	Math	Math	Math	Math	Math
English	English	English	English	English	English
Religion	Religion	Religion	Religion	Religion	Religion
History/Social Studies	History/Social Studies	History/Social Studies	History/Social Studies	History/Social Studies	History/Social Studies
Science	Science	Science	Science	Science	Science

Week 24: Friday, _____
(Date)

Name	Name	Name	Name	Name	Name
Math	Math	Math	Math	Math	Math
English	English	English	English	English	English
Religion	Religion	Religion	Religion	Religion	Religion
History/Social Studies	History/Social Studies	History/Social Studies	History/Social Studies	History/Social Studies	History/Social Studies
Science	Science	Science	Science	Science	Science

Week 25

Memory Scripture Verse

_____

_____

_____

Saint of the Week

_____

Patron of…

_____

I am thankful for…

_____

_____

_____

Grocery List

_____
_____
_____
_____
_____
_____
_____
_____
_____
_____
_____
_____

Meal Planning

Sunday:
_____

Monday:
_____

Tuesday:
_____

Wednesday:
_____

Thursday:
_____

Friday:
_____

Saturday:
_____

"If you believe what you like in the gospels, and reject what you don't like, it is not the gospel you believe, but yourself."

Saint Augustine of Hippo

Week 25: Monday, _____
(Date)

Name	Name	Name	Name	Name	Name
Math	Math	Math	Math	Math	Math
English	English	English	English	English	English
Religion	Religion	Religion	Religion	Religion	Religion
History/Social Studies	History/Social Studies	History/Social Studies	History/Social Studies	History/Social Studies	History/Social Studies
Science	Science	Science	Science	Science	Science

Week 25: Tuesday, _____
(Date)

Name	Name	Name	Name	Name	Name
Math	Math	Math	Math	Math	Math
English	English	English	English	English	English
Religion	Religion	Religion	Religion	Religion	Religion
History/Social Studies	History/Social Studies	History/Social Studies	History/Social Studies	History/Social Studies	History/Social Studies
Science	Science	Science	Science	Science	Science

Week 25: Wednesday, _____

(Date)

Name	Name	Name	Name	Name	Name
Math	Math	Math	Math	Math	Math
English	English	English	English	English	English
Religion	Religion	Religion	Religion	Religion	Religion
History/Social Studies	History/Social Studies	History/Social Studies	History/Social Studies	History/Social Studies	History/Social Studies
Science	Science	Science	Science	Science	Science

Week 25: Thursday, _____
(Date)

Name	Name	Name	Name	Name	Name
Math	Math	Math	Math	Math	Math
English	English	English	English	English	English
Religion	Religion	Religion	Religion	Religion	Religion
History/Social Studies	History/Social Studies	History/Social Studies	History/Social Studies	History/Social Studies	History/Social Studies
Science	Science	Science	Science	Science	Science

Week 25: Friday, _____

(Date)

Name	Name	Name	Name	Name	Name
Math	Math	Math	Math	Math	Math
English	English	English	English	English	English
Religion	Religion	Religion	Religion	Religion	Religion
History/Social Studies	History/Social Studies	History/Social Studies	History/Social Studies	History/Social Studies	History/Social Studies
Science	Science	Science	Science	Science	Science

Week 26

Memory Scripture Verse

_____

_____

_____

Saint of the Week

_____

Patron of…

_____

I am thankful for…

_____

_____

_____

Grocery List

_____
_____
_____
_____
_____
_____
_____
_____
_____
_____
_____
_____
_____
_____

Meal Planning

Sunday:
_____

Monday:
_____

Tuesday:
_____

Wednesday:
_____

Thursday:
_____

Friday:
_____

Saturday:
_____

"Have no anxiety about anything, but in everything by prayer and supplication with thanksgiving let your requests be made known to God."

Philippians 4:6

Week 26: Monday, _____
(Date)

Name	Name	Name	Name	Name	Name
Math	Math	Math	Math	Math	Math
English	English	English	English	English	English
Religion	Religion	Religion	Religion	Religion	Religion
History/Social Studies	History/Social Studies	History/Social Studies	History/Social Studies	History/Social Studies	History/Social Studies
Science	Science	Science	Science	Science	Science

Week 26: Tuesday, _____
(Date)

Name	Name	Name	Name	Name	Name
Math	Math	Math	Math	Math	Math
English	English	English	English	English	English
Religion	Religion	Religion	Religion	Religion	Religion
History/Social Studies	History/Social Studies	History/Social Studies	History/Social Studies	History/Social Studies	History/Social Studies
Science	Science	Science	Science	Science	Science

Week 26: Wednesday, _____

(Date)

Name	Name	Name	Name	Name	Name
Math	Math	Math	Math	Math	Math
English	English	English	English	English	English
Religion	Religion	Religion	Religion	Religion	Religion
History/Social Studies	History/Social Studies	History/Social Studies	History/Social Studies	History/Social Studies	History/Social Studies
Science	Science	Science	Science	Science	Science

Week 26: Thursday, _____

(Date)

Name	Name	Name	Name	Name	Name
Math	Math	Math	Math	Math	Math
English	English	English	English	English	English
Religion	Religion	Religion	Religion	Religion	Religion
History/Social Studies	History/Social Studies	History/Social Studies	History/Social Studies	History/Social Studies	History/Social Studies
Science	Science	Science	Science	Science	Science

Week 26: Friday, _____

(Date)

Name	Name	Name	Name	Name	Name
Math	Math	Math	Math	Math	Math
English	English	English	English	English	English
Religion	Religion	Religion	Religion	Religion	Religion
History/Social Studies	History/Social Studies	History/Social Studies	History/Social Studies	History/Social Studies	History/Social Studies
Science	Science	Science	Science	Science	Science

Week 27

Memory Scripture Verse

Saint of the Week

I am thankful for…

Patron of…

Grocery List

Meal Planning

Sunday:

Monday:

Tuesday:

Wednesday:

Thursday:

Friday:

Saturday:

*"Let nothing disturb you, nothing frighten you;
all things are passing; God never changes."*
St. Teresa of Avila

Week 27: Monday, _____

(Date)

Name	Name	Name	Name	Name	Name
Math	Math	Math	Math	Math	Math
English	English	English	English	English	English
Religion	Religion	Religion	Religion	Religion	Religion
History/Social Studies	History/Social Studies	History/Social Studies	History/Social Studies	History/Social Studies	History/Social Studies
Science	Science	Science	Science	Science	Science

Week 27: Tuesday, _____

(Date)

Name	Name	Name	Name	Name	Name
Math	Math	Math	Math	Math	Math
English	English	English	English	English	English
Religion	Religion	Religion	Religion	Religion	Religion
History/Social Studies	History/Social Studies	History/Social Studies	History/Social Studies	History/Social Studies	History/Social Studies
Science	Science	Science	Science	Science	Science

Week 27: Wednesday, _____

(Date)

Name	Name	Name	Name	Name	Name
Math	Math	Math	Math	Math	Math
English	English	English	English	English	English
Religion	Religion	Religion	Religion	Religion	Religion
History/Social Studies	History/Social Studies	History/Social Studies	History/Social Studies	History/Social Studies	History/Social Studies
Science	Science	Science	Science	Science	Science

Week 27: Thursday, _____

(Date)

Name	Name	Name	Name	Name	Name
Math	Math	Math	Math	Math	Math
English	English	English	English	English	English
Religion	Religion	Religion	Religion	Religion	Religion
History/Social Studies	History/Social Studies	History/Social Studies	History/Social Studies	History/Social Studies	History/Social Studies
Science	Science	Science	Science	Science	Science

Week 27: Friday, _____
(Date)

Name	Name	Name	Name	Name	Name
Math	Math	Math	Math	Math	Math
English	English	English	English	English	English
Religion	Religion	Religion	Religion	Religion	Religion
History/Social Studies	History/Social Studies	History/Social Studies	History/Social Studies	History/Social Studies	History/Social Studies
Science	Science	Science	Science	Science	Science

Week 28

Memory Scripture Verse

_____

_____

_____

Saint of the Week

_____

Patron of…

_____

I am thankful for…

_____

_____

_____

Grocery List

_____
_____
_____
_____
_____
_____
_____
_____
_____
_____
_____
_____

Meal Planning

Sunday:
_____

Monday:
_____

Tuesday:
_____

Wednesday:
_____

Thursday:
_____

Friday:
_____

Saturday:
_____

"To put into practice the teachings of our holy faith, it is not enough to convince ourselves that they are true; we must love them. Love united to faith makes us practice our religion." - St. Alphonsus Liguori

Week 28: Monday, _____
(Date)

Name	Name	Name	Name	Name	Name
Math	Math	Math	Math	Math	Math
English	English	English	English	English	English
Religion	Religion	Religion	Religion	Religion	Religion
History/Social Studies	History/Social Studies	History/Social Studies	History/Social Studies	History/Social Studies	History/Social Studies
Science	Science	Science	Science	Science	Science

Week 28: Tuesday, _____

(Date)

Name	Name	Name	Name	Name	Name
Math	Math	Math	Math	Math	Math
English	English	English	English	English	English
Religion	Religion	Religion	Religion	Religion	Religion
History/Social Studies	History/Social Studies	History/Social Studies	History/Social Studies	History/Social Studies	History/Social Studies
Science	Science	Science	Science	Science	Science

Week 28: Wednesday, _____
(Date)

Name	Name	Name	Name	Name	Name
Math	Math	Math	Math	Math	Math
English	English	English	English	English	English
Religion	Religion	Religion	Religion	Religion	Religion
History/Social Studies	History/Social Studies	History/Social Studies	History/Social Studies	History/Social Studies	History/Social Studies
Science	Science	Science	Science	Science	Science

Week 28: Thursday, _____
(Date)

Name	Name	Name	Name	Name	Name
Math	Math	Math	Math	Math	Math
English	English	English	English	English	English
Religion	Religion	Religion	Religion	Religion	Religion
History/Social Studies	History/Social Studies	History/Social Studies	History/Social Studies	History/Social Studies	History/Social Studies
Science	Science	Science	Science	Science	Science

Week 28: Friday, _____

(Date)

Name	Name	Name	Name	Name	Name
Math	Math	Math	Math	Math	Math
English	English	English	English	English	English
Religion	Religion	Religion	Religion	Religion	Religion
History/Social Studies	History/Social Studies	History/Social Studies	History/Social Studies	History/Social Studies	History/Social Studies
Science	Science	Science	Science	Science	Science

Week 29

Memory Scripture Verse

_____

_____

_____

Saint of the Week

_____

Patron of…

_____

I am thankful for…

_____

_____

_____

Grocery List

_____
_____
_____
_____
_____
_____
_____
_____
_____
_____
_____
_____
_____

Meal Planning

Sunday:
_____

Monday:
_____

Tuesday:
_____

Wednesday:
_____

Thursday:
_____

Friday:
_____

Saturday:
_____

"Joy is a net of love by which we catch souls."

St. Teresa of Calcutta

Week 29: Monday, _____

(Date)

Name	Name	Name	Name	Name	Name
Math	Math	Math	Math	Math	Math
English	English	English	English	English	English
Religion	Religion	Religion	Religion	Religion	Religion
History/Social Studies	History/Social Studies	History/Social Studies	History/Social Studies	History/Social Studies	History/Social Studies
Science	Science	Science	Science	Science	Science

Week 29: Tuesday, _____
(Date)

Name _____	Name _____	Name _____	Name _____	Name _____	Name _____
Math	Math	Math	Math	Math	Math
English	English	English	English	English	English
Religion	Religion	Religion	Religion	Religion	Religion
History/Social Studies	History/Social Studies	History/Social Studies	History/Social Studies	History/Social Studies	History/Social Studies
Science	Science	Science	Science	Science	Science

Week 29: Wednesday, _____

(Date)

Name	Name	Name	Name	Name	Name
Math	Math	Math	Math	Math	Math
English	English	English	English	English	English
Religion	Religion	Religion	Religion	Religion	Religion
History/Social Studies	History/Social Studies	History/Social Studies	History/Social Studies	History/Social Studies	History/Social Studies
Science	Science	Science	Science	Science	Science

Week 29: Thursday, _____
(Date)

Name	Name	Name	Name	Name	Name
Math	Math	Math	Math	Math	Math
English	English	English	English	English	English
Religion	Religion	Religion	Religion	Religion	Religion
History/Social Studies	History/Social Studies	History/Social Studies	History/Social Studies	History/Social Studies	History/Social Studies
Science	Science	Science	Science	Science	Science

Week 29: Friday, _____

(Date)

Name	Name	Name	Name	Name	Name
Math	Math	Math	Math	Math	Math
English	English	English	English	English	English
Religion	Religion	Religion	Religion	Religion	Religion
History/Social Studies	History/Social Studies	History/Social Studies	History/Social Studies	History/Social Studies	History/Social Studies
Science	Science	Science	Science	Science	Science

Week 30

Memory Scripture Verse
_____
_____
_____

Saint of the Week
_____

Patron of…
_____

I am thankful for…
_____
_____

Grocery List

_____
_____
_____
_____
_____
_____
_____
_____
_____
_____
_____
_____
_____
_____

Meal Planning

Sunday:
_____

Monday:
_____

Tuesday:
_____

Wednesday:
_____

Thursday:
_____

Friday:
_____

Saturday:
_____

"Truth always ends by victory; it is not unassailable, but invincible."

St. Ignatius of Loyola

Week 30: Monday, _____

(Date)

Name	Name	Name	Name	Name	Name
Math	Math	Math	Math	Math	Math
English	English	English	English	English	English
Religion	Religion	Religion	Religion	Religion	Religion
History/Social Studies	History/Social Studies	History/Social Studies	History/Social Studies	History/Social Studies	History/Social Studies
Science	Science	Science	Science	Science	Science

Week 30: Tuesday, _____
(Date)

Name	Name	Name	Name	Name	Name
Math	Math	Math	Math	Math	Math
English	English	English	English	English	English
Religion	Religion	Religion	Religion	Religion	Religion
History/Social Studies	History/Social Studies	History/Social Studies	History/Social Studies	History/Social Studies	History/Social Studies
Science	Science	Science	Science	Science	Science

Week 30: Wednesday, _____
(Date)

Name	Name	Name	Name	Name	Name
Math	Math	Math	Math	Math	Math
English	English	English	English	English	English
Religion	Religion	Religion	Religion	Religion	Religion
History/Social Studies	History/Social Studies	History/Social Studies	History/Social Studies	History/Social Studies	History/Social Studies
Science	Science	Science	Science	Science	Science

Week 30: Thursday, _____
(Date)

Name	Name	Name	Name	Name	Name
Math	Math	Math	Math	Math	Math
English	English	English	English	English	English
Religion	Religion	Religion	Religion	Religion	Religion
History/Social Studies	History/Social Studies	History/Social Studies	History/Social Studies	History/Social Studies	History/Social Studies
Science	Science	Science	Science	Science	Science

Week 30: Friday, _____
(Date)

Name	Name	Name	Name	Name	Name
Math	Math	Math	Math	Math	Math
English	English	English	English	English	English
Religion	Religion	Religion	Religion	Religion	Religion
History/Social Studies	History/Social Studies	History/Social Studies	History/Social Studies	History/Social Studies	History/Social Studies
Science	Science	Science	Science	Science	Science

Week 31

Memory Scripture Verse

_____

_____

Saint of the Week

_____

Patron of…

_____

I am thankful for…

_____

_____

Grocery List

_____
_____
_____
_____
_____
_____
_____
_____
_____
_____
_____
_____

Meal Planning

Sunday:
_____

Monday:
_____

Tuesday:
_____

Wednesday:
_____

Thursday:
_____

Friday:
_____

Saturday:
_____

"For pity's sake, don't start meeting troubles halfway."

St. Teresa of Avila

Week 31: Monday, _____

(Date)

Name	Name	Name	Name	Name	Name
Math	Math	Math	Math	Math	Math
English	English	English	English	English	English
Religion	Religion	Religion	Religion	Religion	Religion
History/Social Studies	History/Social Studies	History/Social Studies	History/Social Studies	History/Social Studies	History/Social Studies
Science	Science	Science	Science	Science	Science

Week 31: Tuesday, _____

(Date)

Name	Name	Name	Name	Name	Name
Math	Math	Math	Math	Math	Math
English	English	English	English	English	English
Religion	Religion	Religion	Religion	Religion	Religion
History/Social Studies	History/Social Studies	History/Social Studies	History/Social Studies	History/Social Studies	History/Social Studies
Science	Science	Science	Science	Science	Science

Week 31: Wednesday, _____

(Date)

Name	Name	Name	Name	Name	Name
Math	Math	Math	Math	Math	Math
English	English	English	English	English	English
Religion	Religion	Religion	Religion	Religion	Religion
History/Social Studies	History/Social Studies	History/Social Studies	History/Social Studies	History/Social Studies	History/Social Studies
Science	Science	Science	Science	Science	Science

Week 31: Thursday, _____
(Date)

Name	Name	Name	Name	Name	Name
Math	Math	Math	Math	Math	Math
English	English	English	English	English	English
Religion	Religion	Religion	Religion	Religion	Religion
History/Social Studies	History/Social Studies	History/Social Studies	History/Social Studies	History/Social Studies	History/Social Studies
Science	Science	Science	Science	Science	Science

Week 31: Friday, _____

(Date)

Name	Name	Name	Name	Name	Name
Math	Math	Math	Math	Math	Math
English	English	English	English	English	English
Religion	Religion	Religion	Religion	Religion	Religion
History/Social Studies	History/Social Studies	History/Social Studies	History/Social Studies	History/Social Studies	History/Social Studies
Science	Science	Science	Science	Science	Science

Week 32

Memory Scripture Verse

Saint of the Week

I am thankful for…

Patron of…

Grocery List

Meal Planning

Sunday:

Monday:

Tuesday:

Wednesday:

Thursday:

Friday:

Saturday:

"We know that (God) gives us every grace, every abundant grace; and though we are so weak of ourselves, this grace is able to carry us through every obstacle and difficulty." - St. Elizabeth Ann Seton

Week 32: Monday, _____
(Date)

Name	Name	Name	Name	Name	Name
Math	Math	Math	Math	Math	Math
English	English	English	English	English	English
Religion	Religion	Religion	Religion	Religion	Religion
History/Social Studies	History/Social Studies	History/Social Studies	History/Social Studies	History/Social Studies	History/Social Studies
Science	Science	Science	Science	Science	Science

Week 32: Tuesday, _____
(Date)

Name	Name	Name	Name	Name	Name
Math	Math	Math	Math	Math	Math
English	English	English	English	English	English
Religion	Religion	Religion	Religion	Religion	Religion
History/Social Studies	History/Social Studies	History/Social Studies	History/Social Studies	History/Social Studies	History/Social Studies
Science	Science	Science	Science	Science	Science

Week 32: Wednesday, _____

(Date)

Name	Name	Name	Name	Name	Name
Math	Math	Math	Math	Math	Math
English	English	English	English	English	English
Religion	Religion	Religion	Religion	Religion	Religion
History/Social Studies	History/Social Studies	History/Social Studies	History/Social Studies	History/Social Studies	History/Social Studies
Science	Science	Science	Science	Science	Science

Week 32: Thursday, _____

(Date)

Name	Name	Name	Name	Name	Name
Math	Math	Math	Math	Math	Math
English	English	English	English	English	English
Religion	Religion	Religion	Religion	Religion	Religion
History/Social Studies	History/Social Studies	History/Social Studies	History/Social Studies	History/Social Studies	History/Social Studies
Science	Science	Science	Science	Science	Science

Week 32: Friday, _____
(Date)

Name	Name	Name	Name	Name	Name
Math	Math	Math	Math	Math	Math
English	English	English	English	English	English
Religion	Religion	Religion	Religion	Religion	Religion
History/Social Studies	History/Social Studies	History/Social Studies	History/Social Studies	History/Social Studies	History/Social Studies
Science	Science	Science	Science	Science	Science

Week 33

Memory Scripture Verse

_____

_____

Saint of the Week

_____

Patron of…

_____

I am thankful for…

_____

_____

Grocery List

_____
_____
_____
_____
_____
_____
_____
_____
_____
_____
_____
_____
_____
_____

Meal Planning

Sunday:
_____

Monday:
_____

Tuesday:
_____

Wednesday:
_____

Thursday:
_____

Friday:
_____

Saturday:
_____

"I wish not merely to be called Christian, but also to be Christian."
St. Ignatius of Antioch

Week 33: Monday, _____
(Date)

Name	Name	Name	Name	Name	Name
Math	Math	Math	Math	Math	Math
English	English	English	English	English	English
Religion	Religion	Religion	Religion	Religion	Religion
History/Social Studies	History/Social Studies	History/Social Studies	History/Social Studies	History/Social Studies	History/Social Studies
Science	Science	Science	Science	Science	Science

Week 33: Tuesday, _____

(Date)

Name	Name	Name	Name	Name	Name
Math	Math	Math	Math	Math	Math
English	English	English	English	English	English
Religion	Religion	Religion	Religion	Religion	Religion
History/Social Studies	History/Social Studies	History/Social Studies	History/Social Studies	History/Social Studies	History/Social Studies
Science	Science	Science	Science	Science	Science

Week 33: Wednesday, _____

(Date)

Name	Name	Name	Name	Name	Name
Math	Math	Math	Math	Math	Math
English	English	English	English	English	English
Religion	Religion	Religion	Religion	Religion	Religion
History/Social Studies	History/Social Studies	History/Social Studies	History/Social Studies	History/Social Studies	History/Social Studies
Science	Science	Science	Science	Science	Science

Week 33: Thursday, _____

(Date)

Name	Name	Name	Name	Name	Name
Math	Math	Math	Math	Math	Math
English	English	English	English	English	English
Religion	Religion	Religion	Religion	Religion	Religion
History/Social Studies	History/Social Studies	History/Social Studies	History/Social Studies	History/Social Studies	History/Social Studies
Science	Science	Science	Science	Science	Science

Week 33: Friday, _____

(Date)

Name	Name	Name	Name	Name	Name
Math	Math	Math	Math	Math	Math
English	English	English	English	English	English
Religion	Religion	Religion	Religion	Religion	Religion
History/Social Studies	History/Social Studies	History/Social Studies	History/Social Studies	History/Social Studies	History/Social Studies
Science	Science	Science	Science	Science	Science

Week 34

Memory Scripture Verse

_____

_____

_____

Saint of the Week

_____

Patron of…

_____

I am thankful for…

_____

_____

_____

Grocery List

_____
_____
_____
_____
_____
_____
_____
_____
_____
_____
_____
_____

Meal Planning

Sunday:
_____

Monday:
_____

Tuesday:
_____

Wednesday:
_____

Thursday:
_____

Friday:
_____

Saturday:
_____

"The riddles of God are more satisfying than the solutions of man."
G.K. Chesterton

Week 34: Monday, _____
(Date)

Name	Name	Name	Name	Name	Name
Math	Math	Math	Math	Math	Math
English	English	English	English	English	English
Religion	Religion	Religion	Religion	Religion	Religion
History/Social Studies	History/Social Studies	History/Social Studies	History/Social Studies	History/Social Studies	History/Social Studies
Science	Science	Science	Science	Science	Science

Week 34: Tuesday, _____

(Date)

Name	Name	Name	Name	Name	Name
Math	Math	Math	Math	Math	Math
English	English	English	English	English	English
Religion	Religion	Religion	Religion	Religion	Religion
History/Social Studies	History/Social Studies	History/Social Studies	History/Social Studies	History/Social Studies	History/Social Studies
Science	Science	Science	Science	Science	Science

Week 34: Wednesday, _____

(Date)

Name	Name	Name	Name	Name	Name
Math	Math	Math	Math	Math	Math
English	English	English	English	English	English
Religion	Religion	Religion	Religion	Religion	Religion
History/Social Studies	History/Social Studies	History/Social Studies	History/Social Studies	History/Social Studies	History/Social Studies
Science	Science	Science	Science	Science	Science

Week 34: Thursday, _____

(Date)

Name	Name	Name	Name	Name	Name
Math	Math	Math	Math	Math	Math
English	English	English	English	English	English
Religion	Religion	Religion	Religion	Religion	Religion
History/Social Studies	History/Social Studies	History/Social Studies	History/Social Studies	History/Social Studies	History/Social Studies
Science	Science	Science	Science	Science	Science

Week 34: Friday, _____
(Date)

Name ___	Name ___	Name ___	Name ___	Name ___	Name ___
Math	Math	Math	Math	Math	Math
English	English	English	English	English	English
Religion	Religion	Religion	Religion	Religion	Religion
History/Social Studies	History/Social Studies	History/Social Studies	History/Social Studies	History/Social Studies	History/Social Studies
Science	Science	Science	Science	Science	Science

Week 35

Memory Scripture Verse

_____

_____

_____

Saint of the Week

_____

Patron of…

_____

I am thankful for…

_____

_____

Grocery List

_____
_____
_____
_____
_____
_____
_____
_____
_____
_____
_____
_____
_____
_____

Meal Planning

Sunday:
_____

Monday:
_____

Tuesday:
_____

Wednesday:
_____

Thursday:
_____

Friday:
_____

Saturday:
_____

"Humility is the foundation of all the other virtues hence, in the soul in which this virtue does not exist there cannot be any other virtue except in mere appearance."

Saint Augustine of Hippo

Week 35: Monday, _____
(Date)

Name	Name	Name	Name	Name	Name
Math	Math	Math	Math	Math	Math
English	English	English	English	English	English
Religion	Religion	Religion	Religion	Religion	Religion
History/Social Studies	History/Social Studies	History/Social Studies	History/Social Studies	History/Social Studies	History/Social Studies
Science	Science	Science	Science	Science	Science

Week 35: Tuesday, _____

(Date)

Name	**Name**	**Name**	**Name**	**Name**	**Name**
Math	Math	Math	Math	Math	Math
English	English	English	English	English	English
Religion	Religion	Religion	Religion	Religion	Religion
History/Social Studies	History/Social Studies	History/Social Studies	History/Social Studies	History/Social Studies	History/Social Studies
Science	Science	Science	Science	Science	Science

Week 35: Wednesday, _____
(Date)

Name	Name	Name	Name	Name	Name
Math	Math	Math	Math	Math	Math
English	English	English	English	English	English
Religion	Religion	Religion	Religion	Religion	Religion
History/Social Studies	History/Social Studies	History/Social Studies	History/Social Studies	History/Social Studies	History/Social Studies
Science	Science	Science	Science	Science	Science

Week 35: Thursday, _____

(Date)

Name	Name	Name	Name	Name	Name
Math	Math	Math	Math	Math	Math
English	English	English	English	English	English
Religion	Religion	Religion	Religion	Religion	Religion
History/Social Studies	History/Social Studies	History/Social Studies	History/Social Studies	History/Social Studies	History/Social Studies
Science	Science	Science	Science	Science	Science

Week 35: Friday, _____

(Date)

Name ___	Name ___	Name ___	Name ___	Name ___	Name ___
Math	Math	Math	Math	Math	Math
English	English	English	English	English	English
Religion	Religion	Religion	Religion	Religion	Religion
History/Social Studies	History/Social Studies	History/Social Studies	History/Social Studies	History/Social Studies	History/Social Studies
Science	Science	Science	Science	Science	Science

Week 36

Memory Scripture Verse

_____

_____

_____

Saint of the Week

_____

Patron of…

_____

I am thankful for…

_____

_____

_____

Grocery List

_____
_____
_____
_____
_____
_____
_____
_____
_____
_____
_____
_____

Meal Planning

Sunday:
_____

Monday:
_____

Tuesday:
_____

Wednesday:
_____

Thursday:
_____

Friday:
_____

Saturday:
_____

"The world's thy ship and not thy home."

St. Thérèse of Lisieux

Week 36: Monday, _____
(Date)

Name	Name	Name	Name	Name	Name
Math	Math	Math	Math	Math	Math
English	English	English	English	English	English
Religion	Religion	Religion	Religion	Religion	Religion
History/Social Studies	History/Social Studies	History/Social Studies	History/Social Studies	History/Social Studies	History/Social Studies
Science	Science	Science	Science	Science	Science

Week 36: Tuesday, _____
(Date)

Name	Name	Name	Name	Name	Name
Math	Math	Math	Math	Math	Math
English	English	English	English	English	English
Religion	Religion	Religion	Religion	Religion	Religion
History/Social Studies	History/Social Studies	History/Social Studies	History/Social Studies	History/Social Studies	History/Social Studies
Science	Science	Science	Science	Science	Science

Week 36: Wednesday, _____

(Date)

Name	Name	Name	Name	Name	Name
Math	Math	Math	Math	Math	Math
English	English	English	English	English	English
Religion	Religion	Religion	Religion	Religion	Religion
History/Social Studies	History/Social Studies	History/Social Studies	History/Social Studies	History/Social Studies	History/Social Studies
Science	Science	Science	Science	Science	Science

Week 36: Thursday, _____

(Date)

Name	Name	Name	Name	Name	Name
Math	Math	Math	Math	Math	Math
English	English	English	English	English	English
Religion	Religion	Religion	Religion	Religion	Religion
History/Social Studies	History/Social Studies	History/Social Studies	History/Social Studies	History/Social Studies	History/Social Studies
Science	Science	Science	Science	Science	Science

Week 36: Friday, _____

(Date)

Name	Name	Name	Name	Name	Name
Math	Math	Math	Math	Math	Math
English	English	English	English	English	English
Religion	Religion	Religion	Religion	Religion	Religion
History/Social Studies	History/Social Studies	History/Social Studies	History/Social Studies	History/Social Studies	History/Social Studies
Science	Science	Science	Science	Science	Science

Calendars & Planning Pages

Let the Children Come Unto Me by C. Vogelstein

AUGUST 2018

Sunday	Monday	Tuesday	Wednesday	Thursday	Friday	Saturday
			1	2	3 First Friday	4 First Saturday
5	6	7	8	9	10	11
12	13	14	15	16	17	18
19	20	21	22	23	24	25
26	27	28	29	30	31	

Selected Feast Days:

August 4: Saint John Vianney
August 6: The Transfiguration of the Lord
August 8: Saint Dominic
August 11: Saint Clare
August 14: Saint Maximilian Kolbe

August 15: The Assumption of the Blessed
    Virgin Mary (Holy Day of Obligation)
August 22: The Queenship of Mary
August 27: Saint Monica
August 28: Saint Augustine of Hippo

What I want to accomplish:

_____

_____

_____

What I want my children to accomplish:

_____

_____

_____

Spiritual goals for the month:

_____

_____

_____

Special activities:

_____

_____

_____

SEPTEMBER 2018

Sunday	Monday	Tuesday	Wednesday	Thursday	Friday	Saturday
						1 First Saturday
2	3	4	5	6	7 First Friday	8
9	10	11	12	13	14	15
16	17	18	19	20	21	22
23	24	25	26	27	28	29
30						

Selected Feast Days:

September 8: The Birth of the Blessed Virgin Mary
September 14: The Exaltation of the Holy Cross
September 15: Our Lady of Sorrows
September 19: Saint Januarius
September 23: Saint Padre Pio
September 29: Saints Michael, Gabriel, and Raphael
September 30: Saint Jerome

What I want to accomplish:

_____

_____

_____

What I want my children to accomplish:

_____

_____

_____

Spiritual goals for the month:

_____

_____

_____

Special activities:

_____

_____

_____

OCTOBER 2018

Sunday	Monday	Tuesday	Wednesday	Thursday	Friday	Saturday
	1	2	3	4	5 First Friday	6 First Saturday
7	8	9	10	11	12	13
14	15	16	17	18	19	20
21	22	23	24	25	26	27
28	29	30	31			

Selected Feast Days:

October 1: Saint Thérèse of Lisieux
October 2: The Holy Guardian Angels
October 4: St. Francis of Assisi
October 5: Saint Faustina
October 7: Our Lady of the Rosary

October 15: Saint Teresa of Avila
October 17: Saint Margaret Mary Alacoque
October 22: Saint John Paul II
October 28: Saints Simon and Jude

What I want to accomplish:

_____
_____
_____

What I want my children to accomplish:

_____
_____
_____

Spiritual goals for the month:

_____
_____
_____

Special activities:

_____
_____
_____

NOVEMBER 2018

Sunday	Monday	Tuesday	Wednesday	Thursday	Friday	Saturday
				1	2 First Friday	3 First Saturday
4	5	6	7	8	9	10
11	12	13	14	15	16	17
18	19	20	21	22 Thanksgiving	23	24
25	26	27	28	29	30	

Selected Feast Days:

November 1: All Saints Day (Holy Day of
               Obligation)
November 2: All Souls Day
November 11: Saint Martin of Tours
November 13: Saint Frances Xavier Cabrini
November 17: Saint Elizabeth of Hungary

November 21: The Presentation of the
               Blessed Virgin Mary
November 22: Thanksgiving
November 25: Our Lord Jesus Christ,
               King of the Universe
November 30: Saint Andrew

What I want to accomplish:

_____

_____

_____

What I want my children to accomplish:

_____

_____

_____

Spiritual goals for the month:

_____

_____

_____

Special activities:

_____

_____

_____

DECEMBER 2018

Sunday	Monday	Tuesday	Wednesday	Thursday	Friday	Saturday
						1 First Saturday
2	3	4	5	6	7 First Friday	8
9	10	11	12	13	14	15
16	17	18	19	20	21	22
23	24	25 Christmas	26	27	28	29
30	31					

Selected Feast Days:

December 2: First Sunday of Advent
December 6: Saint Nicholas
December 8: Immaculate Conception of the
  Blessed Virgin Mary (Holy Day of Obligation)
December 9: Saint Juan Diego

December 12: Our Lady of Guadalupe
December 25: The Nativity of the Lord
  (Holy Day of Obligation)
December 26: Saint Stephen
December 28: The Holy Innocents

What I want to accomplish:

_____

_____

_____

What I want my children to accomplish:

_____

_____

_____

Spiritual goals for the month:

_____

_____

_____

Special activities:

_____

_____

_____

JANUARY 2019

Sunday	Monday	Tuesday	Wednesday	Thursday	Friday	Saturday
		1	2	3	4 First Friday	5 First Saturday
6	7	8	9	10	11	12
13	14	15	16	17	18	19
20	21	22	23	24	25	26
27	28	29	30	31		

Selected Feast Days:
January 1: Mary, the Holy Mother of God
                (Holy Day of Obligation)
January 4: Saint Elizabeth Ann Seton
January 6: Epiphany
January 24: Saint Francis de Sales

January 25: The Conversion of Saint
                Paul
January 28: Saint Thomas Aquinas
January 31: Saint John Bosco

What I want to accomplish:

_____

_____

_____

What I want my children to accomplish:

_____

_____

_____

Spiritual goals for the month:

_____

_____

_____

Special activities:

_____

_____

_____

FEBRUARY 2019

Sunday	Monday	Tuesday	Wednesday	Thursday	Friday	Saturday
					1 First Friday	2 First Saturday
3	4	5	6	7	8	9
10	11	12	13	14	15	16
17	18	19	20	21	22	23
24	25	26	27	28		

Selected Feast Days:
February 2: The Presentation of the Lord
February 3: Saint Blaise
February 11: Our Lady of Lourdes
February 22: The Chair of Saint Peter

What I want to accomplish:

_____

_____

_____

What I want my children to accomplish:

_____

_____

_____

Spiritual goals for the month:

_____

_____

_____

Special activities:

_____

_____

_____

MARCH 2019

Sunday	Monday	Tuesday	Wednesday	Thursday	Friday	Saturday
					1 First Friday	2 First Saturday
3	4	5	6	7	8	9
10	11	12	13	14	15	16
17	18	19	20	21	22	23
24	25	26	27	28	29	30
31						

Selected Feast Days:

March 6: Ash Wednesday
March 7: Saints Perpetua and Felicity
March 17: Saint Patrick
March 19: Saint Joseph

What I want to accomplish:

_____

_____

_____

What I want my children to accomplish:

_____

_____

_____

Spiritual goals for the month:

_____

_____

_____

Special activities:

_____

_____

_____

APRIL 2019

Sunday	Monday	Tuesday	Wednesday	Thursday	Friday	Saturday
	1	2	3	4	5 First Friday	6 First Saturday
7	8	9	10	11	12	13
14	15	16	17	18	19	20
21 Easter	22	23	24	25	26	27
28	29	30				

Selected Feast Days:
April 14: Palm Sunday
April 19: Good Friday
April 21: Easter Sunday
April 28: Divine Mercy Sunday

What I want to accomplish:

_____

_____

_____

What I want my children to accomplish:

_____

_____

_____

Spiritual goals for the month:

_____

_____

_____

Special activities:

_____

_____

_____

MAY 2019

Sunday	Monday	Tuesday	Wednesday	Thursday	Friday	Saturday
			1	2	3 First Friday	4 First Saturday
5	6	7	8	9	10	11
12 Mother's Day	13	14	15	16	17	18
19	20	21	22	23	24	25
26	27	28	29	30	31	

Selected Feast Days:
May 1: St. Joseph the Worker
May 13: Our Lady of Fátima
May 15: St. Dymphna
May 16: St. Simon Stock
May 22: St. Rita of Cascia
May 30: The Ascension of the Lord (Holy Day of Obligation, transferred to Sunday, June 2 in most U.S. dioceses)

What I want to accomplish:

_____

_____

_____

What I want my children to accomplish:

_____

_____

_____

Spiritual goals for the month:

_____

_____

_____

Special activities:

_____

_____

_____

JUNE 2019

Sunday	Monday	Tuesday	Wednesday	Thursday	Friday	Saturday
						1 First Saturday
2	3	4	5	6	7 First Friday	8
9	10	11	12	13	14	15
16 Father's Day	17	18	19	20	21	22
23	24	25	26	27	28	29
30						

Selected Feast Days:

June 9: Pentecost
June 13: Saint Anthony of Padua
June 16: Trinity Sunday

June 20: Corpus Christi
June 28: Sacred Heart of Jesus
June 29: Saints Peter and Paul

What I want to accomplish:

___

___

___

What I want my children to accomplish:

___

___

___

Spiritual goals for the month:

___

___

___

Special activities:

___

___

___

JULY 2019

Sunday	Monday	Tuesday	Wednesday	Thursday	Friday	Saturday
	1	2	3	4 Independence Day	5 First Friday	6 First Saturday
7	8	9	10	11	12	13
14	15	16	17	18	19	20
21	22	23	24	25	26	27
28	29	30	31			

Selected Feast Days:
July 3: Saint Thomas the Apostle
July 6: Saint Maria Goretti
July 11: Saint Benedict of Nursia
July 14: Saint Kateri Tekakwitha
July 15: Saint Bonaventure
July 16: Our Lady of Mount Carmel
July 22: Saint Mary Magdalene
July 26: Saints Joachim and Anne
July 29: Saint Martha
July 31: Saint Ignatius of Loyola

What I want to accomplish:

_____

_____

_____

What I want my children to accomplish:

_____

_____

_____

Spiritual goals for the month:

_____

_____

_____

Special activities:

_____

_____

_____

Curriculum List

Student **Subject** **Title**

_____

_____

_____

_____

_____

_____

_____

_____

_____

_____

Curriculum List

Student   Subject   Title

Reading List

Student   **Title**   **Author**

Reading List

Student Title Author

Reading List

Student   Title   Author

Reading List

Student　　　　　　　　Title　　　　　　　　Author

Field Trips

Place   Date   Time

_____

_____

_____

_____

_____

_____

_____

_____

Goals for Next Year

Grades for _____

Subject	1st Quarter	2nd Quarter	3rd Quarter	4th Quarter	Final Grade

Grades for _____

Subject	1st Quarter	2nd Quarter	3rd Quarter	4th Quarter	Final Grade

Grades for _____

Subject	1st Quarter	2nd Quarter	3rd Quarter	4th Quarter	Final Grade

Grades for _____

Subject	1st Quarter	2nd Quarter	3rd Quarter	4th Quarter	Final Grade

Grades for _____

Subject	1st Quarter	2nd Quarter	3rd Quarter	4th Quarter	Final Grade

Grades for _____

Subject	1st Quarter	2nd Quarter	3rd Quarter	4th Quarter	Final Grade

Catholic Prayers

The Prayer by William-Adolphe Bouguereau

The Our Father
Our Father who art in Heaven, hallowed be Thy name; Thy Kingdom come; Thy will be done on earth as it is in Heaven. Give us this day our daily bread; and forgive us our trespasses as we forgive those who trespass against us; and lead us not into temptation, but deliver us from evil. Amen.

The Hail Mary
Hail Mary, full of grace! The Lord is with thee; blessed art thou among women, and blessed is the fruit of thy womb, Jesus. Holy Mary, Mother of God, pray for us sinners, now and at the hour of our death. Amen.

The Glory Be
Glory be to the Father, and to the Son, and to the Holy Spirit. As it was in the beginning, is now, and ever shall be, world without end. Amen.

The Fatima Prayer
O my Jesus, forgive us our sins, save us from the fires of hell, and lead all souls to Heaven, especially those most in need of Thy mercy. Amen.

Hail, Holy Queen
Hail, holy Queen, mother of mercy, our life, our sweetness, and our hope. To thee do we cry, poor banished children of Eve. To thee do we send up our sighs mourning and weeping in this valley of tears. Turn then, most gracious advocate, thine eyes of mercy toward us, and after this our exile show us the blessed fruit of thy womb, Jesus.
O clement, O loving, O sweet Virgin Mary.
Pray for us, O Holy Mother of God.
That we may be made worthy of the promises of Christ.

Grace Before Meals
Bless us, O Lord, and these Thy gifts, which we are about to receive from Thy bounty, through Christ our Lord. Amen.

Grace After Meals
We give Thee thanks for all your benefits, O Almighty God, Who lives and reigns forever; and may the souls of the faithful departed, through the mercy of God, rest in peace. Amen.

Memorare
Remember, O most gracious Virgin Mary, that never was it known that anyone who fled to thy protection, implored thy help, or sought thine intercession was left unaided.
Inspired by this confidence, I fly unto thee, O Virgin of virgins, my mother; to thee do I come, before thee I stand, sinful and sorrowful. O Mother of the Word Incarnate, despise not my petitions, but in thy mercy hear and answer me. Amen.

The Guardian Angel Prayer
Angel of God, my guardian dear, to whom God's love commits me here, ever this day be at my side to light and guard, to rule and guide. Amen.

The Act of Contrition

O my God, I am heartily sorry for having offended Thee, and I detest all my sins, because I dread the loss of Heaven and the pains of Hell; but most of all because they offend Thee, my God, Who art all good and deserving of all my love. I firmly resolve, with the help of Thy grace, to confess my sins, to do penance and to amend my life. Amen.

The Divine Praises

Blessed be God.
Blessed be His Holy Name.
Blessed be Jesus Christ, true God and true Man.
Blessed be the Name of Jesus.
Blessed be His Most Sacred Heart.
Blessed be His Most Precious Blood.
Blessed be Jesus in the Most Holy Sacrament of the Altar.
Blessed be the Holy Spirit, the Paraclete.
Blessed be the great Mother of God, Mary most holy.
Blessed be her holy and Immaculate Conception.
Blessed be her glorious Assumption.
Blessed be the name of Mary, Virgin and Mother.
Blessed be St. Joseph, her most chaste spouse.
Blessed be God in His angels and in His saints.

The Morning Offering

O Jesus, through the Immaculate Heart of Mary, I offer You my prayers, works, joys and sufferings of this day for all the intentions of Your Sacred Heart, in union with the Holy Sacrifice of the Mass throughout the world, in reparation for my sins, for the intentions of all my relatives and friends, and in particular for the intentions of the Holy Father. Amen.

Prayer to Saint Michael the Archangel

Saint Michael the Archangel, defend us in battle. Be our defense against the wickedness and snares of the Devil. May God rebuke him, we humbly pray, and do thou, O Prince of the Heavenly hosts, by the power of God, thrust into hell Satan, and all the evil spirits, who prowl about the world seeking the ruin of souls. Amen.

The Creed

I believe in God, the Father almighty, Creator of Heaven and earth, and in Jesus Christ, His only Son, our Lord. He was conceived by the Holy Spirit, and born of the Virgin Mary.
He suffered under Pontius Pilate, was crucified, died, and was buried. He descended into hell. On the third day He rose again. He ascended into Heaven, and is seated at the right hand of God the Father Almighty. He will come again to judge the living and the dead.
I believe in the Holy Spirit, the Holy Catholic Church, the communion of saints, the forgiveness of sins, the resurrection of the body, and life everlasting. Amen.

The Holy Rosary

1. Make the Sign of the Cross and say, "In the name of the Father, and of the Son, and of the Holy Spirit. Amen."

2. Say the Creed, one Our Father, three Hail Marys, and one Glory Be.

3. Announce the first Mystery. Then pray one Our Father, ten Hail Marys, one Glory Be, and one Fatima Prayer while meditating on the Mystery.

4. Then pray one Our Father, ten Hail Marys, one Glory Be, and one Fatima Prayer for each Mystery.

5. After you have completed all the decades, say the Hail, Holy Queen.

6. Make the Sign of the Cross and say, "In the Name of the Father, and of the Son, and of the Holy Spirit. Amen."

Joyful Mysteries

1. The Annunciation

2. The Visitation

3. The Nativity

4. The Presentation

5. The Finding of Jesus in the Temple

Sorrowful Mysteries

1. Agony in the Garden

2. Scourging at the Pillar

3. Crowning with Thorns

4. Carrying of the Cross

5. The Crucifixion

Luminous Mysteries

1. Baptism in the Jordan

2. The Wedding Feast at Cana

3. Proclamation of the Kingdom

4. The Transfiguration

5. Institution of the Eucharist

Glorious Mysteries

1. The Resurrection

2. The Ascension

3. The Descent of the Holy Spirit

4. Assumption of the Blessed Virgin Mary

5. Coronation of the Blessed Virgin Mary

The 15 Promises of the Holy Rosary

The Blessed Mother gave Saint Dominic and Blessed Alan de la Roche promises that she assured them were given to those who recite the Holy Rosary faithfully.

Here are the promises:

1. Whosoever shall faithfully serve me by the recitation of the Rosary shall receive signal graces.

2. I promise my special protection and the greatest graces to all those who shall recite the Rosary.

3. The Rosary shall be a powerful armor against hell; it will destroy vice, decrease sin and defeat heresies.

4. It will cause good works to flourish; it will obtain for souls the abundant mercy of God; it will withdraw the hearts of men from the love of the world and its vanities, and will lift them to the desire for Eternal Things. Oh, that souls would sanctify themselves by this means.

5. The soul which recommends itself to me by the recitation of the Rosary shall not perish.

6. Whosoever shall recite the Rosary devoutly, applying himself to the consideration of its Sacred Mysteries shall never be conquered by misfortune. God will not chastise him in His justice; he shall not perish by an unprovided death; if he be just he shall remain in the grace of God, and become worthy of Eternal Life.

7. Whoever shall have a true devotion for the Rosary shall not die without the Sacraments of the Church.

8. Those who are faithful to recite the Rosary shall have during their life and at their death the Light of God and the plenitude of His Graces; at the moment of death they shall participate in the Merits of the Saints in Paradise.

9. I shall deliver from Purgatory those who have been devoted to the Rosary.

10. The faithful children of the Rosary shall merit a high degree of Glory in Heaven.

11. You shall obtain all you ask of me by recitation of the Rosary.

12. All those who propagate the Holy Rosary shall be aided by me in their necessities.

13. I have obtained from my Divine Son that all the advocates of the Rosary shall have for intercessors the entire Celestial Court during their life and at the hour of death.

14. All who recite the Rosary are my Sons, and brothers of my Only Son Jesus Christ.

15. Devotion to my Rosary is a great sign of predestination.

Quotes about the Holy Rosary

"The Rosary is a powerful weapon to put the demons to flight and to keep oneself from sin…. If you desire peace in your hearts, in your homes and in your country, assemble each evening to recite the Rosary. Let not even one day pass without saying it, no matter how burdened you may be with many cares and labors."
Pope Pius XI

"How beautiful is the family that recites the Rosary every evening."
Saint John Paul II
-

"Among all the devotions approved by the Church none has been so favored by so many miracles as the devotion of the Most Holy Rosary."
Blessed Pius IX

"You always leave the Rosary for later, and you end up not saying it at all because you are sleepy. If there is no other time, say it in the street without letting anybody notice it.
It will, moreover, help you to have presence of God."
Saint Josemaria Escriva

"The Rosary is the 'weapon' for these times."
Saint Padre Pio

"When people love and recite the Rosary, they find it makes them better."
Saint Anthony Mary Claret

"Say the Rosary every day to obtain world peace."
Our Lady of Fátima

"There is no problem, I tell you, no matter how difficult it is, that we cannot solve by the prayer of the Holy Rosary."
Sister Lúcia de Jesus Rosa dos Santos (seer of Fátima)

"If you say the Rosary faithfully until death, I do assure you that, in spite of the gravity of your sins, you shall receive a never-fading crown of glory. Even if you are on the brink of damnation… sooner or later you will be converted and will amend your life and will save your soul, if – and mark well what I say – if you say the Holy Rosary devoutly every day until death for the purpose of knowing the truth and obtaining contrition and pardon for your sins."
Saint Louis de Montfort

The Divine Mercy Chaplet

Step 1 – Using a Rosary, begin at the cross by making the Sign of the Cross.

(Optional Opening Prayer)
You expired, Jesus, but the source of life gushed forth for souls, and the ocean of mercy opened up for the whole world. O Fount of Life, unfathomable Divine Mercy, envelop the whole world and empty Yourself out upon us.

Step 2 - O Blood and Water, which gushed forth from the Heart of Jesus as a fountain of Mercy for us, I trust in You! (Repeat three times)

Step 3 – On the three beads of the Rosary, pray the Our Father, the Hail Mary, and the Apostles' Creed.

Step 4 – Begin each decade with the Our Father beads by praying this prayer:

Eternal Father, I offer You the Body and Blood, Soul and Divinity of Your dearly beloved Son, Our Lord Jesus Christ, in atonement for our sins and those of the whole world.

Step 5 – Complete the decade on the 10 Hail Mary beads by praying this prayer:

For the sake of His Sorrowful Passion, have mercy on us and on the whole world.

Repeat steps 4 and 5 for each decade.

Step 6 – After praying all five decades, pray the following prayer 3 times:

Holy God, Holy Mighty One, Holy Immortal One, have mercy on us and on the whole world.

Step 7 – (Optional Closing Prayer)
Eternal God, in whom mercy is endless and the treasury of compassion inexhaustible, look kindly upon us, and increase Your mercy in us, that in difficult moments, we might not despair nor become despondent, but with great confidence, submit ourselves to Your holy will, which is Love and Mercy itself. Amen.

The 12 Promises of the Sacred Heart of Jesus

We can practice devotion to the Sacred Heart of Jesus by displaying His Sacred Heart prominently in our homes, having our houses Consecrated to the Sacred Heart, and by making the Nine First Fridays in honor of Jesus' Sacred Heart. The following are the promises that Jesus gave to Saint Margaret Mary Alacoque for those who are devoted to His Sacred Heart:

1. I will give them all the graces necessary in their state of life.

2. I will give peace in their families and will unite families that are divided.

3. I will console them in all their troubles.

4. I will be their refuge during life and above all in death.

5. I will bestow the blessings of Heaven on all their enterprises.

6. Sinners shall find in my Heart the source and infinite ocean of mercy.

7. Tepid souls shall become fervent.

8. Fervent souls shall rise quickly to great perfection.

9. I will bless those places wherein the image of My Heart shall be exposed and honored and will imprint My love on the hearts of those who would wear this image on their person. I will also destroy in them all disordered movements.

10. I will give to priests who are animated by a tender devotion to my Divine Heart the gift of touching the most hardened hearts.

11. Those who promote this devotion shall have their names written in my Heart, never to be effaced.

12. I promise you in the excessive mercy of my Heart that my all-powerful love will grant to all those who communicate on the First Friday in nine consecutive months, the grace of final penitence: they will not die in my disgrace, nor without receiving their Sacraments. My Divine Heart shall be their safe refuge in this last moment.

The Seven Sorrows Chaplet

According to St. Bridget of Sweden's (1303-1373) visions, the Blessed Virgin promised to grant seven graces to those who meditate daily on her Sorrows:

- "I will grant peace to their families."
- "They will be enlightened about the divine Mysteries."
- "I will console them in their pains and will accompany them in their work."
- "I will give them as much as they ask for as long as it does not oppose the adorable will of my divine Son or the sanctification of their souls."
- "I will defend them in their spiritual battles with the infernal enemy, and I will protect them at every instant of their lives."
- "I will visibly help them at the moment of their death-- they will see the face of their mother."
- "I have obtained this grace from my divine Son, that those who propagate this devotion to my tears and dolors will be taken directly from this earthly life to eternal happiness, since all their sins will be forgiven and my Son will be their eternal consolation and joy."

How to Pray the Seven Sorrows (Dolors) Chaplet:

Step 1 – (Optional) Make an Act of Contrition

Step 2 – Pray one Our Father and seven Hail Marys for each of Mary's Sorrows.

The First Sorrow: The Prophecy of Simeon (Luke 2:25-35)

The Second Sorrow: The Flight Into Egypt (Matthew 2:13-15)

The Third Sorrow: The Child Jesus Lost in the Temple (Luke 2:41-50)

The Fourth Sorrow Mary Meeting Jesus as He Carries the Cross

The Fifth Sorrow Mary at the Foot of the Cross (John 19:25-30)

The Sixth Sorrow Mary receives the Body of Jesus

The Seventh Sorrow: Jesus' Burial (Luke 23:50-56)

Step 3 – Pray three Hail Marys in honor of the Blessed Mother's Tears. Pray one Our Father, Hail Mary, and one Glory Be for the Holy Father's intentions. Finally, pray "Virgin Most Sorrowful, Pray for Us" three times.

Regular Prayer Intentions

I am thankful for...

_____

_____

_____

_____

_____

_____

_____

_____

_____

_____

Daily Checklist

In my experience, it is helpful to have a list of memorization items to read out-loud to my children each day. This list includes prayers, the names of the Apostles, children's full names and birthdays, ABCs, numbers, the presidents, states and capitals, our address and phone number, left and right, and the list could go on forever. Here is a place where you can list all of your daily memory items.

- _____
- _____
- _____
- _____
- _____
- _____
- _____
- _____
- _____
- _____
- _____
- _____
- _____
- _____
- _____
- _____
- _____
- _____
- _____
- _____
- _____
- _____

- _____
- _____
- _____
- _____
- _____
- _____
- _____
- _____
- _____
- _____
- _____
- _____
- _____
- _____
- _____
- _____
- _____
- _____
- _____
- _____
- _____
- _____

Notes

Books by Jennifer and Travis Rainey

A Catholic Prayer Journal for Kids

A Catholic Prayer Journal for Moms

A Catholic Prayer Journal

A Catholic Mom's Guide to Starting a Home Business

The Busy Mom's Meal Planning Journal

My Advent Journey (coming October 2018)

2019 Catholic Planner (coming October 2018)

My Lenten Journey 2019 (coming early 2019)

If you join my email list, I will send you a free electronic copy of *A Catholic Prayer Journal*. Just send me an email: Webmaster@ourcatholiccorner.com. I will not send more than twelve emails each year.

Thank you so much, and may God bless you!

Made in the USA
Columbia, SC
27 July 2018